CALL ME BITTER

DEVOTIONS FOR THE HURTING

Dr. Lee Ann B. Marino, Ph.D., D.Min., D.D.

Call Me Bitter
Devotions For The Hurting

Dr. Lee Ann B. Marino, Ph.D., D.Min., D.D.

Published by:

Remnant Words

(An imprint of the Righteous Pen Publications Group)
www.righteouspenpublications.com

All rights reserved. Except as permitted under the U.S. Copyright Act of 1976, no part of this book may be reproduced, distributed, or transmitted in any form or by any means, electronic or mechanical, or saved in any information storage and retrieval system without written permission from the author.

Unless otherwise indicated, all Scripture quotations are taken from **the Amplified® Bible, Classic Edition** Copyright © 1954, 1958, 1962, 1964, 1965, 1987 by The Lockman Foundation. Used by permission." (www.Lockman.org)

Scripture quotations marked (NIV) are taken from the **Holy Bible, New International Version®, NIV®.** Copyright © 1973, 1978, 1984, 2011 by Biblica, Inc.™ Used by permission of Zondervan. All rights reserved worldwide. www.zondervan.com. The "NIV" and "New International Version" are trademarks registered in the United States Patent and Trademark Office by Biblica, Inc.™

All passages marked KJV are from the **King James Version of the Holy Bible**, Public Domain.

Book classification: 1. Nonfiction > Religion > Christian Life > Death, Grief, Bereavement

Copyright © 2022 by Lee Ann B. Marino.

ISBN: 1-940197-66-X
13-Digit: 978-1-940197-66-1

Printed in the United States of America.

And when your fears subside
And shadows still remain, oh yeah
I know that you can love me
When there's no one left to blame
So never mind the darkness,
We still can find a way
'Cause nothin' lasts forever,
Even cold November rain
(Guns N' Roses)'

TABLE OF CONTENTS

	Word from the Author	1
1	The Wrong Words at the Wrong Time	1
2	Leaving Things Alone	5
3	Call Me Bitter	9
4	Facing Everyday Life When You Want to Face Nothing	13
5	Hurting in Front of Everyone	17
6	Life in Contradictions	21
7	Screw-Up	25
8	Trying Too Hard	29
9	Because Hope Hurts	33
10	All Feelings Matter	37
11	Dark, But Lovely	41
12	Damaged	45
13	How I Didn't Get Over	49
14	Human, All-Too-Human	53
15	Blessed Silence	57
16	The God Who Sees My Misery	61
17	Mourning in the Abstract	65
18	There is Hope for a Tree	69
19	The Space Between	73
20	When You Hurt…But Can't Tell Anyone	77
21	Roses	81
22	Comfort Me	85
23	Resolution	89
24	I'm Not OK and That's OK	93
25	Beautifully Broken	97
26	Dry Places	101
27	Brave Endings	105
28	Stop Waiting for Friday	109
	Afterword	113
	References	117
	Other Books of Interest By the Author	119
	About the Author	121

WORD FROM THE AUTHOR

AND [HANNAH] WAS IN DISTRESS OF SOUL, PRAYING TO THE LORD AND WEEPING BITTERLY. (1 SAMUEL 1:10)

STRONG'S #04843 – מָרַר: MÂRAR; TO BE BITTER; TO SHOW BITTERNESS; TO MAKE BITTER; EMBITTER; TO EMBITTER ONESELF; TO BE ENRAGED; TO BE STRONG, STRENGTHEN[2]

SOME books are introduced; some need explaining. Others, still, require a combination of both. This book, I believe, rests in that combination. Here we have both a reflection and personal journey as I have wrestled, for the past several months to stop waiting for a magical moment to come along that will make me "feel better" ...whatever that even means. In the aftermath of my husband's death, discord with his family, moving, losing a beloved dog, gallbladder problems, a disaster retreat event, and then the COVID-19 lockdowns and restrictions in 2020 and 2021, I found myself feeling the deep emptiness caused by loss more than I had at any other time in the past two-and-a-half years prior.

If this wasn't enough, I began a long – and often traumatic – emotional and mental journey through my eleven-year marriage. Trauma, memories, and long-stored emotional wounds came back, often in increments. I'd go from angry to grief-stricken to traumatized in a matter of a few hours to days, only to find myself back at the place of emptiness. A few cycles of this later, I was officially in a place I would classify as bitter. Happy couples, engagements, dating failures (of which I had more than one), bad days, feeling overlooked and invisible, moving again (and the stress that went along with that), changes in relationships with friends, and life in general left me with a sense of dark, brooding melancholy boiling over with anger, hurt, and resentment.

All of a sudden, I started identifying with Bible characters who had what we might classify as "bitter" experiences. The primary one was Naomi, who was so moved by her bitter experience she desired people call her Mara, meaning "bitter." Much like she, and other Biblical characters felt at points in their lives, I also struggle (even now) with feeling like life has nothing more to offer. It had to be I either had something great ahead or had nothing, and I bounced between these two extremes for months, hoping something would materialize to help me feel better or at least different than I was feeling.

It was in this darkness that I struggled with binary, either/or concepts that kept me waiting for something external to rescue me from the emotional landslide that never seemed to stop. I thought I had to be magically better, in a different place, to feel better. The mentalities that my relationship had to be all one way or the other, that I had to feel one way or another, and that I had to have outlooks one way or another all crushed me under the weight of confusing and complex emotions that didn't get any better.

I was walking my dog, Gideon one day when I got the idea for this book. I recalled Naomi's emotional state and her desired name change from "pleasant" to "bitter" due to her experience. In the four chapters of Ruth, we learn that Naomi went from bitter to pleasant again through a process that was her own. She started, as the word "bitter" entails, embittered. She ended strengthened by her own journey, one that was hers as much as it was Ruth's. It didn't happen because she "positive confessed" her way out of her life, through denial, or by thinking good thoughts; it came about because her life changed, one day at a time. While she waited for that change to come, she stayed in her dark, bitter place, working to survive.

The Bible never criticizes Naomi (or other Bible characters, for that matter) for her emotional struggle. She was never minimized or bullied for not being a positive thinker or told that her faith was insufficient. She moved through the different phases of her immediate grief because she wasn't pushed into an "either/or" binary box. There was no question she could be bitter and have faith, move forward and still grieve her loss, and experience days where she felt empty and still hope for better days to come. Naomi didn't experience either/or; she lived in both/and. She found her strength in her bitterness, because it gave her the ability to see life in a full picture.

As I started writing this book, I realized my "either/or" thinking was driving me head-first into worse emotional territory. I assumed mental and emotional health mean never having any "negative" feelings. I concerned myself my faith wasn't where it needed to be because I so strongly felt the deep bitterness that set itself over my life. I feared I was unpleasant when around others. My mind swirled and twisted and moved among dark, complicated emotions, lacing them with new concerns. Instead of just letting myself be where I was, I kept trying to fix it.

I have experienced a bitter deal on many fronts. The past few years of my life have changed me. It's unreasonable to expect that, with the different events that have taken place, I can be the same person I once was. Whether or not this change is positive or negative isn't the consequence; it is a fact. Things are different than they used to be. At some point in time, they will, most likely, change again. My life won't be what it once was; somewhere in here, I am working to make that adjustment. Sometimes the change comes through different feelings and views about life, but in other ways, I believe many of my underlying thoughts and feelings have often been magnified and validated. It takes time to relearn something else, especially when new things creep in and validate older things. It's not as simple, nor solved, by hoping something else will take it away.

Instead of feeling pressure to be someone else, I am – slowly – learning to embrace my own personal bitterness, darkness, and melancholy. None of it makes me a bad person or an unbelieving person. It just means this is part of where I am at, whether it remains for a season, or on some level, as part of my outlook for the rest of my life. I am learning how to be OK with being me, whoever that might be on any given day, no matter how dark that day might be. I face every one of my bitter days. I survive them, learning to take new approaches as I see life differently. And as someone recently told me to take all the time I need, that is exactly what I am going to do.

My deepest hope is to find the place where bitterness turns to strength, as is found in the definition. It happened for Naomi, Ruth, Hannah, Job, and the long list of others in Scripture who found strength in their bitter places. I no longer see these concepts in binary terms, however. Their bitterness made them strong because in bitterness, we find strength. There, we learn to feel, to embrace the bad as much as we try to avoid it, and to feel the darkness that bitterness often brings. We know how to weather life. And with it, there is the realization that it's not going to be an experience of binaries, but one that is non-binary: life will bring times of bitter again, times of strength, and times of both, at once.

It's OK to be both/and. It's OK to not be OK. It's OK to have a bad day. It's OK to feel. Ouch. Yes, it's OK to feel, even the hard feelings. It's OK to feel good sometimes. It's OK to laugh. It's OK to be dark and bitter, and brood in that space. It's OK to embrace it all, whenever and however it comes.

I thank everyone who has – and who continues – to listen, to be there, even when I'm as tired of feeling it as they are of hearing it. Most of all, I thank those in my life – the members of Sanctuary International Fellowship Tabernacle (SIFT), both in North Carolina and Kentucky; my mom, Nina, my besties, Julie, Brian, Nik, Charlie, John, and Lyle; and last, but certainly not least, everyone who loves me enough to help me get through the day – for offering all those moments that make my life feel a little less bitter.

ONE

THE WRONG WORDS AT THE WRONG TIME

> Let your speech at all times be gracious (pleasant and winsome), seasoned [as it were] with salt, [so that you may never be at a loss] to know how you ought to answer anyone [who puts a question to you].
> (Colossians 4:6)

Reading: James 3:1-6

ONE day I was sitting at the table with someone when she uttered the wrong words in my general direction at the absolute wrong time.

"Some things are just lessons for us —"

I promptly interrupted her at that point. I didn't care if I came across as rude or improper. I couldn't go through this conversation again.

"Don't say that to me again."

Two days earlier, she'd said the same exact thing to me. I was reiterating how an event I held eight months earlier sent me into an emotional spiral. The response I had to the event's circumstances left me believing I was not a good leader and no longer suited for ministry. This event was the last in a long string of things that had seemed to attack me for well over two years. First, I questioned whether I wanted to be in ministry. Second, my late husband got very sick and then died shortly after. I had to leave my home and the area where I lived for ten years. I was diagnosed with gallbladder disease after a severe gallbladder attack and surgery was discussed. Then my dog of ten years became very ill and died shortly after her initial onset. Within four months of her death, COVID-19 hit, sending us all into quarantine.

    I had reservations about hosting the event, but I looked forward to seeing people I hadn't seen in a long time. I thought maybe the event would help us with a COVID year that changed plans and left us feeling lost and empty. When the event turned out to be a disaster in ways I was not prepared to handle, it added an entirely new component to the complex sense of impossibility and doom that already lurked over my life. There was no silver lining, no bright, shiny sun behind the dark clouds that seemed to hang over my head. I didn't need a lesson. I didn't want to be taught anything. I definitely didn't want to feel like this whole thing was to teach me some abstract thing. I was hurting. I needed someone to acknowledge that.

    When we go through things that leave us with hurt, it can feel like everyone has an opinion about our situation. They aren't necessarily words or thoughts designed to hurt us...but somehow, they often do. Others hope to make us see our situation differently. They give us the "busy work" of "self-improvement" in a trying situation: if we see the bright side of things, we will feel different.

    We've heard it all: "Things will get better!" "Some things are lessons for us to learn." "Just think of all the people you'll be able to help who go through the same thing!" "Things will happen for you, at the right time." These lines make us scan our minds for their meaning: when will they get better? What lessons? Who cares about helping anyone else right now? Why do I need a "right time" to feel better?

The wrong words don't help. Sometimes, all we need is a quiet, comforting reality: something that tells us it's all right to hurt, without trying to fix it with wrong words. Presence helps us know we are not alone. When we hurt, words aren't enough...and the wrong words are definitely not needed. Presence, however, is always just what we need.

If bitterness wants to get into the act,
I offer it a cookie or a gumdrop.
(James Broughton)[3]

TWO

Leaving Things Alone

In the multitude of my [anxious] thoughts within me, Your comforts cheer AND delight my soul!
(Psalm 94:19)

Reading: Matthew 11:25-30

I have crazy, kinky curly hair that can't make up its mind as to what it wants to do. When I was very young, my hair was fine and straight, like what I would perceive "normal hair" on myself to be. When I reached a certain age, it started to curl...and curl...and it has been downhill ever since. My dreams of being a girl with long, straight black hair would never be a reality. Instead, I have hair that hairdressers don't want to cut (several of which butchered my head), that weights down with the wrong shampoo or conditioner, easily tangles, and must be either styled in a specific way or left alone to its own devices: to God and the elements.

On a day-to-day basis, it is impractical for me to try and style my hair. It is too time consuming and cuts into my sleep quality. As a result, I have learned to try and master "wash and wear" hair with a head full of hair that just doesn't want to "wear" the same way two days in a row. I never know quite what it is going to do, how it is going to curl, or what it is going to morph into that day. It's like gambling with my head, only in a way that can make me look like anything from Buckwheat to Marilyn Monroe.

For many years, I "over-fussed" my hair as part of

my daily routine. If it was wet, I would repeatedly comb it in the hopes it would flip the way I wanted it to go. Every time I'd notice it going some way that didn't look like I thought it should as it would dry, I'd try to comb it in the way I wanted it to go. At one stage in the drying process, my hair looks awful, no matter what I might try to do to it, tempting me even more to fuss, and fuss, and fuss some more. I would try, with many vain efforts, to force it into submission, hoping it would look other than it did.

Whenever I would fuss with my hair, it would look awful once it dried completely. Then one day, I decided that maybe instead of fussing with it, I should leave it alone to do its own thing. I avoided the mirror during the particularly unattractive phase of its drying process and let it be, brushing it only when nearly or completely dry. The transformation was amazing: it looked like I had normal hair that set just the right way for its antics that day, rather than trying to force it into a hairdo that it wasn't made to suit at that time.

From this experience, I learned the valuable lesson in leaving some things alone. I wasn't doing myself any favors by trying to get my hair to do something it wasn't made to do. All I did was cause myself unnecessary frustration.

Much like my hair, grief and hurt tend to do whatever it is they are going to do. We can try to push ourselves out of our states of being, but it is far better to sometimes just let them be what they are, leaving them — and us — alone to mend in our own time. The more we touch, the more we hurt; the more we feel less like ourselves, and the more disconnected from the person we want to become.

Learning to leave things alone is one of the greatest gifts we can give ourselves. It is part of the process of acceptance, of learning to accept things we cannot change because we cannot control them. This is where freedom begins, hard as it often is to achieve. It allows us the space for rest. It gives us the opportunity to receive the natural process of change, as time will move within us. It gives us space and breath and self-care. Most importantly, though, it gives us time to listen to the sound of silence that assures us peace can be found through the storm that rages within our lives.

> Custom turns everything upside down. Give it time, and what can resist its hardening effect? What does not yield to use? How many find that the bitterness they had formerly dreaded has, unfortunately, through use alone, turned to sweetness?
> (Bernard of Clairvaux)[4]

THREE

CALL ME BITTER

> So they both went on until they came to Bethlehem. And when they arrived in Bethlehem, the whole town was stirred about them, and said, Is this Naomi? And she said to them, Call me not Naomi [pleasant]; call me Mara [bitter], for the Almighty has dealt very bitterly with me. I went out full, but the Lord has brought me home again empty. Why call me Naomi, since the Lord has testified against me, and the Almighty has afflicted me?
> (Ruth 1:19-21)

Reading: Job 10:1-12

WHEN I was first widowed, I identified strongly with Ruth. Ruth, as a young Biblical widow, experienced the sting of living and working hard as she was forced into a life she never saw coming. Even now, I still do identify with her: I live with a much older person, the entirety of my life's course has switched around, and I am forced to do everything necessary to survive. I'm sure that in dark hours, Ruth wrestled much like I have: with her own feelings, her own sense of loss, and her own remarkable way of coming to terms with her new life and its complications.

We tend to paint Ruth as an impossibly cheerful, optimistic Biblical character. I know firsthand that wasn't her reality. It's not realistic to assume she saw her life in such an upbeat way. Ruth, like all young widows, saw her life through a different lens: one that altered her perception of herself, her abilities, and who she was yet to become as a person.

I remember the day when I started identifying with another character in the story though, one that most don't find so optimistic or honorable: Naomi. In particular, I related to Naomi's extreme feeling of bitterness: bitter to the point where she felt it proper and appropriate to rename herself: from "Naomi," which means "pleasant," to "Mara," which means, "bitter."

Major wow moment...Naomi didn't deny her feelings. She didn't call how she felt anything other than what it was. Naomi's life outlook felt dark and bleak; and she owned it, like a boss. She made no compromise in acknowledging she didn't believe it could improve, not even for a moment. She felt that deeply bitter life, the results of bitter experiences and bitter emotions. In those moments, she felt like she would never, ever be happy or joyful again.

People talk a lot about bitterness as if people who experience it choose to be embittered and angry, hating the whole world. Bitterness doesn't feel like an assault on the happiness of others, however. What bitterness really feels like is an intense, discontented heaviness; an awareness that life can be all-too-often cruel and cold, taking something away and leaving nothing in its place. It is a form of deep sorrow, one that can only be described as an embitterment towards life and any possibility of better to come. Bitterness develops because life doesn't seem to offer anything good. When one lives like this long enough, it's easy to reach the point where one believes life has nothing good to offer, ever again.

When it comes to teaching about bitterness, our purpose shouldn't be to label or offend the hurting. This makes them feel worse than they already do, magnifying the narrative that life will never be good or hopeful again. What we should aim to do is find that compassionate heart, to empathize and listen, and let those embittered by life feel a true sense of comfort and inspiration in their experience. In bitterness, the anecdote is presence...not excessive words or judgments. Ruth and Naomi offered one another this comfort, one that was most often had, probably not in what was said, but what wasn't said as the days, weeks, and months passed from bitter to hopeful, once again.

Naomi's unashamed bitterness is a part of the story we are often uncomfortable confronting. If we don't confront it, however, we will never realize bitterness is part of life. It is an uncomfortable part, but a necessary response to the unfairness life sometimes offers. At some point, it always comes knocking. When it does, own it like a boss, just like Naomi did.

FROM THE VERY FOUNTAIN OF ENCHANTMENT
THERE ARISES A TASTE OF BITTERNESS
TO SPREAD ANGUISH AMONGST THE FLOWERS.
(LUCRETIUS)[5]

FOUR

FACING EVERYDAY LIFE WHEN YOU WANT TO FACE NOTHING

> THERE IS NOTHING BETTER FOR A MAN
> THAN THAT HE SHOULD EAT AND DRINK AND MAKE
> HIMSELF ENJOY GOOD IN HIS LABOR. EVEN THIS,
> I HAVE SEEN, IS FROM THE HAND OF GOD. FOR WHO CAN
> EAT OR WHO CAN HAVE ENJOYMENT ANY MORE
> THAN I CAN—*APART FROM HIM*?
> (ECCLESIASTES 2:24-25)

READING: LUKE 10:38-42

I worked all day. It wasn't a typical eight-hour day, but one that creeped dangerously into the 13-hour zone. Getting through the day was hard enough: it was filled with things that already took an immense amount of effort...like getting out of bed...taking a shower...preparing food...editing a lousy manuscript someone else wrote...looking on social media...answering emails...returning a phone call...and teaching a class. I wanted to do none of it. I wanted to stay in the comfort of my bed, where hurting didn't seem to hurt quite so much.

Instead, I got up and did everything I was expected to do.

Then, there was the laundry. It was the infamous laundry that made it from the washer to the dryer, and now needed to be put away...somewhere. I'd faced things all day; now I had to face that laundry, too. It was too much. It was overbearing. I told myself I was being ridiculous, but I just couldn't face the laundry.

For the first time in my nearly forty years of life, I considered becoming a nudist. Doing so would mean I'd have one less thing to deal with in my life: laundry. Whereby I had made it through the whole day dealing with things, the laundry was the one thing I just felt like I couldn't face. In response, I turned off the light, backed out of the room, and pretended I had no concept of laundry, because such didn't exist in my realm of existence.

The laundry was the thing that became my focus. If I was to be honest, I didn't want to do anything I did that day. I was having a terrible time facing everyday life because I wanted to face nothing. I found myself easily bored and overall disinterested in the things I had to do. I hated what I did day-to-day, but I forced myself to continue doing it. Hate it or not, if I started doing without it, I'd have to face the vast, engulfing emptiness that was swallowing up my existence. I felt like I was going nowhere, with nothing ahead and now nothing to hold close as the emptiness turned to a fading black over my life.

Hurt, grief, and loss have a way of making us feel like we aren't good enough. It echoes somewhere within us: if we were better at something, or did something different, or were someone else, this wouldn't have happened to us. Our minds naturally go to the place of self-blame, thinking that if we would just not be...us...we would not hurt.

Such thinking leads us to feel it is not worth the effort to do anything for a good while. We must relearn how to want to do things: how to find satisfaction in everyday life and completion of ordinary tasks, because we are busy being emotionally cautious. We worry if we do or like something too much, we might wind up right where we are again, forever.

Though we want to do nothing, we need to find balance between doing too much and too little. Doing nothing all the time is the last thing that will benefit us. It is important to maintain routine, even when we hurt. We will still feel a sense of accomplishment when we do a good job or complete a task, and that goes a long way to make us feel human again.

Wash the dish. Do the laundry. Clean. Read. Do your work. Take a break. Find your balance.

BITTER LOVE IS BETTER THAN SWEET HATE.
(MATSHONA DHILWAYO)[6]

FIVE

Hurting in Front of Everyone

> For it seems to me that God has made an exhibit of us apostles, exposing us to view last [of all, like men in a triumphal procession who are] sentenced to death [and displayed at the end of the line]. For we have become a spectacle to the world [a show in the world's amphitheater] with both men and angels [as spectators].
> (1 Corinthians 4:9)

Reading: Romans 5:1-8

It was one thing when the first guy didn't get back to me. I still felt all right; maybe he was just very busy and forgot about me, at least temporarily. Then it was a second, and a third, and so on, until it literally became every single person I even considered going out with, except for two. One of the two lasted about four months long distance until it wasn't feasible anymore. The other one had behaviors I could see easily turning abusive, so I backed away. Everyone else had this bad habit of vanishing before anything started.

The "vanishing act" wasn't always one or two dates and done. Most of the time, there were a few conversations that led to the request for an in-person date or meeting. A date would be set, it was discussed we would do something specific, and then I wouldn't hear from that individual again. On a few occasions, someone would pop up again, tell me why they disappeared, very eloquently state the reasons it had nothing to do with me, pledge to do better and promise to do things differently...and then do the same thing all over again.

Dating again after my husband's death was difficult enough. It was hard to have to talk about myself to potential interests, navigating the confusing world of online dating sites made my head spin, and fielding inappropriate comments felt like a contact sport. There were older men, there were men my own age, there were younger men, then there were much younger men... which wasn't something I anticipated happening for me and caused a great deal of soul searching and inward chaos. The experience left me exhausted, confused, and raw. I didn't know how I felt about any of it.

The thing that hurt worse than being consistently ditched was having to tell other people I was being consistently ditched. The first time wasn't bad. It gave us the chance to muse over how awful men are and voice complaints we all had with the modern dating experience. Over time, however, these conversations became less entertaining. It didn't help that in the meantime, one of the women in our group started seeing someone she liked, and they became an official "couple." The "men suck" conversations turned into unhelpful dating advice that left me feeling put on the spot and embarrassed. Having to tell people over and over again that the same thing kept happening (no matter what I did differently) left me feeling ashamed.

We can never underestimate the importance of community support when we are dealing with difficult times. It's important to realize, though, that some things will trigger us, even from those who care about us the most. It's hard to hurt in front of other people, no matter how much they may love us. This becomes more complicated when their situations have changed and they've forgotten or don't know how difficult it can be to stand alone, hurting, in your immediate circumstances.

    Hurting in front of others is not easy. It feels like all eyes are on you and everyone knows (without empathy) what you are going through. You experience feelings that range from exposure to judgment, to feeling like no one understands. Then we have those moments where someone connects, and we know someone understands. Then we realize just how glad we were to talk about whatever we are going through. To get to the one, sometimes we go through the group...so the one will know we hurt.

So bitter is the taste in my mouth,
when I remember making that choice.
(Kristy McGinnis)[7]

SIX

LIFE IN CONTRADICTIONS

But [in apparent contradiction to all this] You [even You the faithful Lord] have cast off and rejected; You have been full of wrath against Your anointed. You have despised *and* loathed and renounced the covenant with Your servant; You have profaned his crown by casting it to the ground. You have broken down all his hedges *and* his walls; You have brought his strongholds to ruin.
(Psalm 89:38-40)

READING: HABAKKUK 3:1-6

I want comfort. I want to be left alone. I want attention. I want to be invisible. I want to be acknowledged. I want to feel unnoticed. I want to be included. I don't want to go out. I want things to make sense. I am still confused. I want more of life. I want to sit over here while life passes me by.

I used to be an "either-or" person, like most in this world. I thought I had to be one thing or the other all the time. Anything but "either-or" was unacceptable. This was reinforced through the advice I was often given, especially in times of confusion: "Make up your mind!" I was given the clear message that to have my "mind made up" or have a set direction, I couldn't have more than one thought, feeling, or desire at a time. It had to be one thing, one feeling, one concept, one idea, one experience for it to count. Anything else was considered chaotic, inappropriate, confused, or distracted.

When we hurt, we are suddenly faced with what I call "life in contradictions." Whereas we have heard most, if not all our lives, facing more than one thing at a time will lead to some cataclysmic disaster... hurt brings the magnifies the reality that we live with contradictions all the time. While we struggle through life with the vain hope of trying to remain without contradiction, hurt makes us realize contradiction is part of human experience.

Sometimes I think we try too hard to force life to make good sense. We want life, life's circumstances, our feelings, and outlook to all line up like ducks in a row for the taking. When this doesn't happen, we don't know what to make of it. Suddenly, nothing makes sense. It assaults our very concept of life as a singular, ordered principle.

Hurt is one of those things that doesn't make sense. It causes us to feel a million different thoughts, emotions, and conflicts all at once, while we are forced to carry on with our everyday lives. We no longer have the convenient illusion that life only happens one thing at a time. Now we manage our thoughts, feelings, fears, and yes, contradictions, all at once. We learn that hurt has a million or more different manifestations and we can feel every single one of them in the time it takes us to fold the laundry, take a shower, or finish dinner.

Hurt is a challenge beyond what we imagine because it calls us out of our comfort zones in more ways than any of us can adequately talk about. We can't easily explain how we want contradictory things or feel contradictory things... and still we do. Hurt forces us to live these contradictions and realize that while things might not make sense, they are still a reality. We grow more at ease with the fact that life is not always "either-or," but more often than not, "both/and."

In a strange way, hurt helps us better embrace and accept "life on life's terms," as we describe such in Twelve Step programs. We face the fact that life isn't just one thing. We are not just one thing. Somehow, we bring ourselves together, so we are better able to manage all things that come our way. It's not always pretty and doesn't look like we expect it should, but we get through. Through hurt, I have come to embrace the phenomenal ball of contradictions that grace my life, because it's all right when things just don't make sense.

> Those bitter memories felt like a wrongly inked tattoo; it sticks to me adamantly even when I want to get rid of it.
> (Misbah Khan)[8]

SEVEN

Screw-Up

> FOR A RIGHTEOUS MAN FALLS SEVEN TIMES
> AND RISES AGAIN, BUT THE WICKED
> ARE OVERTHROWN BY CALAMITY.
> (PROVERBS 24:16)

Reading: Romans 8:1-4

I have a strong tendency to be a perfectionist. There are all sorts of theories about how such behavior emerges in life: from growing up as the child of an addict (check), to never feeling like I quite measured up (check), to feeling chronically overshadowed and as if I was never "good enough" (check, check). My thinking, I suppose, is that if I could just get it perfect and do everything exactly in the right way, things would be different. I don't know that "different" has a specified identity, other than saying I wouldn't feel like a total mess any longer. I would finally measure up, get my just do, and feel "good enough." I've spent a good portion of my life aspiring for that moment when I will no longer feel second, third, or fourth best. I'd give my all to everything I could and hoped for the day when my aspirations of perfection would finally pay off.

I've never achieved my anticipated day full of perfect aspirations. Instead, I wound up in an emotional state of being engulfed in hurt; hurt that was, in many ways, unspeakable and easily misunderstood by others. As thing after thing after thing seemed to fall apart, it was obvious perfection was unobtainable. This led me to feel worse than even fourth best; it made me feel like a total screw-up. I felt like I couldn't do anything right. Everything was falling apart, and there was no way to stop the tidal wave of collapse that enveloped my life. I couldn't prevent it, nor could I put it back together. I had to let everything fall apart and sit in my reality: I had screwed everything up. This magnified over my entire life: I felt like I had screwed up my whole existence. Nothing of it could be fixed, or corrected, ever again.

If this sounds a little melodramatic, it probably was. The hurt I experienced made it seem larger than life, impossible-to-manage, and like nothing was going to be good, ever again. At the same time, I needed to embrace this aspect of myself, even if it made me hurt worse than I already felt. I needed to feel like a screw-up because that feeling broke through the sense of perfection I aimed to achieve. Perfection was never going to be. The only way I could fully realize this was if I felt like I could do nothing right...so I would stop trying.

It was an abasing reality, one that swung between extremes to make a sobering point. I couldn't be a perfectionist, at least in this situation. No amount of perfection could fix things that were over. Feeling like a screw-up would keep me from trying to touch situations that needed space and time to heal, much like I did, too. I needed to stop trying to make things different than they were...and accept them.

The world gives us the impression that "giving up" is a bad thing. If something isn't right, we should apply more effort, more pressure, or do something different to change it. I'd say it's good for us to give things a chance and to do what we can when we are able to do such in any possible situation. Things don't always work out this way, however. Sometimes we have to do what we need to do, take our hands off of things, and let the process work itself out without our pesky need to interfere with things like perfection.

So, here I sit, and I wait, and I feel as I do. I feel like a screw-up, so I'll release myself from trying to fix it unto an abstract sense of perfection, and let God do what He does best: restore.

PATIENCE IS BITTER,
BUT ITS FRUIT IS SWEET.
(JEAN-JACQUES ROUSSEAU)[9]

EIGHT

TRYING TOO HARD

> [JOB'S FRIENDS] ARE AMAZED *AND* EMBARRASSED,
> THEY ANSWER NO MORE; THEY HAVE NOT A THING TO SAY
> [REPORTS ELIHU]. AND SHALL I WAIT, BECAUSE THEY
> SAY NOTHING BUT STAND STILL AND ANSWER NO MORE?
> I ALSO WILL ANSWER MY [GOD-ASSIGNED] PART;
> I ALSO WILL DECLARE MY OPINION *AND* MY KNOWLEDGE.
> FOR I AM FULL OF WORDS; THE SPIRIT WITHIN ME
> CONSTRAINS ME.
> (JOB 32:15-18)

READING: PSALM 88:1-13

JOB is one of those Bible characters most avoid until they have an experience that causes them to identify with him. The sudden way in which Job is hit with unspeakable calamity strikes a chord in those who've been hit with intense loss, grief, suffering...or all three. Job spent the duration of his experience asking why, seeking God when the limits of human wisdom failed him. His long-winded discourses with the Most High were more than prayers; they were demands of explanation as his mind raced for reasons why he suffered as he did. God was the only One Job could talk to about these deeper questions, wrought through existential crisis. Job's story is one of not understanding: when you scan things over and only resort to the question "why" because nothing makes any sense.

Job wasn't the only one who didn't understand what he was going through. Not even Job's wife could relate to his situation. Instead of retorting with a list of reasons why Job was a huge pain of a husband and offer that his suffering could make him a better man, her answer was he should curse God and die. Then there were Job's friends: Eliphaz, Bildad, and Zophar. They too came around with unhelpful advice. Eliphaz suggested Job was being punished for his sins. Bildad suggested he was suffering so he could get something better. Zophar believed Job's experience was divinely arbitrary. They all mused, monologuing instead of dialoging, with words that caused Job to feel worse than he already did.

Let's give Job's friends some credit. These were, after all, Job's friends; not his enemies. They did show up to be there for their friend in his hard time. They offered the best thoughts they had to offer as his friends, recognizing his suffering. As sincere as they might have been, Job's friends made one crucial mistake: they tried too hard to explain his situation. They tried so hard, they were no longer emotionally present with Job. Their focus became their thoughts and ideas about suffering, pain, and the greater meaning of life than the fact that their friend was hurting.

It's very common to experience people who mean well, but "try too hard" when one is hurting. Sure, they don't mean any harm, but too much talk about the "bigger picture" of suffering is not the best idea when suffering becomes personal. Job's experience with suffering wasn't universal as he went through it (even though it would become so later with its inclusion in Biblical literature). The loss, the grief, the feelings of emptiness and angst, and the overall sense of "Why is this happening to me?" required more than distant, objective detachment. Job needed his friends to be present with him, listening and supportive, rather than untimely amateur philosophers.

I believe it is difficult to be there for people in suffering for the very reason that watching someone go through something so trying makes these deeper issues personal for all of us. We like the idea of suffering as a distant musing, something that happens to other people without touching us too close. When it does get too close, we try too hard to push it away. In the process, we push the hurting further away. Suffering is not the time to make life a teachable moment. Some situations, some feelings, some experiences require empathy, not instruction. That empathy may save a friendship, rather than create a rebuke.

Life would pall if it were all sugar;
salt is bitter if taken by itself;
but when tasted as part of the dish,
it savours the meat.
Difficulties are the salt of life.
(Robert Baden-Powell)[10]

NINE

BECAUSE HOPE HURTS

> Rejoice with those who rejoice [sharing others' joy], and weep with those who weep [sharing others' grief]. Live in harmony with one another; do not be haughty (snobbish, high-minded, exclusive), but readily adjust yourself to [people, things] *and* give yourselves to humble tasks. Never overestimate yourself *or* be wise in your own conceits.
> (Romans 12:15-16)

Reading: Psalm 10:14-18

In a first-season episode of the hit show *Greenleaf*, Bishop Greenleaf and his daughter, Pastor Grace Greenleaf make a hospital visit to a family in need of prayer and pastoral care. Bishop Greenleaf fell back on his familiar "preaching style" methods of platitude encouragement. He was quick to tell them to be and think positive, to believe for the best, and to trust that things would be all right. Pastor Grace, seeing what he was doing, took him aside and told him that in such situations, hope can hurt. It was a time where such encouragements and ideas might sound helpful, but they aren't. Nobody needs bolstering in that moment. In contrast, they need a calm, steady presence to remind them God is with them, and they aren't alone.

When I was often at my most bitter and lowest of places, people wanted to offer "hope." It would often come in the form of unhelpful suggestions, words to try and look at the "bright side" of things or maybe reframe the experience in some way. You know, things that are said to us as if we never thought about them before? At a certain point, these suggestions became more than just unhelpful; they became hurtful. They hurt because they echoed on things I already tried to tell myself in the hopes they would push me out of my own thoughts and feelings and into something else, without success. The more I tried to figure it out, tried to force myself to feel any way other than I was feeling, the less hopeful I felt. The "hope" didn't make me feel hopeful; it made me hurt.

Sometimes circumstances don't present a bright side when we examine them in the present. There is no silver lining to the clouds that darken the horizon and prevent the sun from breaking through. The idea that a better day lies ahead — even if we know such will sometime come from a rational perspective — is too hard to fathom. The feelings, emotions, process of hurt or grief is so overwhelming, there isn't room for much else. All we can do is hurt and wait for the time when the pain breaks long enough for light to shine through.

We like to fast-track people through hurt and pain, deeming such as "negative emotions," with the intention of making ourselves feel more comfortable. The hurt and pain of others make us realize there will come a time in life when we, too, will hurt (or reminds us of a hurt or pain that isn't quite as resolved as we hoped it would be by this time). It's not realistic to expect that others won't hurt so we won't have to deal with our own grief. As one who has been on the other side of that, it invites the sense that people don't know and don't care what it's like to hurt...making things hurt even more.

Hurting people don't need a cute saying. We cannot force anyone to find hope when there is none for them to find. The church needs to receive the message that process isn't a sin. It's all right to be going through, however long that lasts. Faith is a walk not just for the feelings that inspire positivity and hope; it is also there for those that are dark and hopeless, that demand one finds the introspection of growth and insight. In such times, the support of believers should be to stand with those who mourn, praying and embracing the dark veil that wisdom often wears.

    Sometimes hope hurts because sometimes life hurts. Hope might hurt, life might hurt, but support is one thing that should never hurt as we comfort those who mourn.

I THINK YOU HAVE TO PAY FOR LOVE WITH BITTER TEARS.
(EDITH PIAF)"

TEN

ALL FEELINGS MATTER

JESUS WEPT.
(JOHN 11:35)

READING: PSALM 147:1-4

IF you have any knowledge of the Bible, you've most likely heard the story of the resurrection of Lazarus. Story has it that Lazarus became ill and died. When he was sick, Martha and Mary (Lazarus' sisters) sent word to Jesus about the situation. Calm and rational (as Jesus usually was), He didn't drop everything. He continued the work at hand for another two days. Instead of running to Lazarus' bedside, Jesus spoke to the disciples about resurrection. This wasn't a concept foreign to them, but none of them had seen a resurrection firsthand. When Jesus sought to return, Lazarus had been dead for four days. When He came to the tomb, the Bible tells us Jesus wept with Mary over the loss of her brother.

Have you ever stopped to wonder why the Bible includes this detail? To the reader, Jesus crying over the loss of a man He is about to bring back from the dead doesn't seem to make sense. It's obvious Jesus knew Lazarus was going to die and He knew that he would rise again immediately, rather than having to wait until the end of time to see him. So why did Jesus cry? Was He swept up in Mary's tide of emotion? Was He trying to fit in with those around Him? Was it a matter of custom?

It was none of these things. Jesus was sending the

clear and distinct message that all feelings matter. "Positive" feelings aren't more important than "negative" ones. Whether those feelings last for a few moments (as was Jesus' situation) or for a longer period (as when we are called to bind the brokenhearted), there are no "wrong" feelings. Jesus didn't stand at the grave of a dead friend with His dead friend's sister and tell her to cheer up or turn a negative situation into a positive one. Instead, He stood there and felt the pain of that moment. He grieved, not for her in pity, but with her.

When my late husband died, I felt an overwhelming sense of dismissal from those I knew. His family treated me as if my feelings didn't matter, as if I wasn't sad that he died. People I knew grew distant and often talked about a "better day" when I would feel like a new person. Some even told me that I needed to get on with my life within a short time of his death. It felt awful. It felt like no one cared. It felt like my feelings didn't matter, a message I'd already received throughout my life. While people might have thought they were doing the right thing to try and help me move forward, they were giving me the dangerous message that I didn't matter because my feelings didn't matter.

God is just as much God when we hurt as when we don't. God has the power to heal, save, raise, and deliver in any situation, but that doesn't mean He doesn't consider our feelings about whatever might be happening. Sometimes we don't see a grand miracle because God sits beside us and weeps, just like we see at the tomb of Lazarus. Jesus wasn't so mighty or powerful that he would dismiss someone's hurt, nor was He too lofty to feel His own grief. This is why Hebrews speaks of us having a High Priest who understands: Jesus was in touch with the human experience, knowing how painful life can be sometimes. Instead of dismissing life's hurt, He sat down and wept, too.

The God of all creation cares enough about each and every feeling we have to grieve with us instead of leaving us to feel such things alone. In this, we can take comfort: all feelings matter to God – even the hard ones – because we matter to Him.

ONE HAS TO SWALLOW A BITTER PILL TO GET CURED.
(SHARAD PAWAR)[12]

ELEVEN

Dark, But Lovely

> Dark am I, yet lovely,
> daughters of Jerusalem,
> dark like the tents of Kedar,
> like the tent curtains of Solomon.
> (Song of Solomon 1:5, NIV)

Reading: Lamentations 3:21-24

THE Song of Solomon is a controversial book of Scripture, for one glaring reason: it's an intense love song between a couple. Their conversation is graphic, to say the least: they discuss in detail their attraction to one another, the way they feel about the other's looks, personality, and physical attributes. This tends to be the main focus of this epic love song as people get so hung up on its thorough and descriptive nature. There is an important aspect of the Song of Solomon, however, that we often ignore. The long-winded poems don't just talk about physical issues. In a few spots, they also address deep-seated issues of insecurity and identity crisis.

The woman in the Song of Solomon details her experiences mistreated and abused by men; first detailing forced hard labor, tending to the fields of her stepbrothers instead of her own; second, speaking of patriarchal control over her; third, with an attack by watchmen that resulted in rape. Within the society and culture where she lived, she had plenty of reasons to feel ashamed or like she was second class. The most outstanding issue she faced was the way in which her long history of abuse and violence would make it difficult for her to marry. Much like today, what happened to her was deemed "her fault" within her culture. Who would love her with such a stained history?

The thing I most love about the woman in the Song of Solomon is how forward she was. She was upfront, personally and sexually, about her intent. She owned how she felt, her desires (which is amazing in light of her history), and also her past. There's no lie in saying she was "dark" for more than one reason, even if the immediate context was sun damaged skin from laboring in her stepbrothers' fields. She was "dark" because her experience was dark. Her world was dark: it was marred by mistreatment and unspeakable hurt that changed her. She couldn't undo or erase it, because trauma was part of her reality. In this, she declared who she was to the world: Dark, but lovely.

We don't like the message that trauma can have life-long implications. We like the idea of being all right "in spite of" trauma, grief, pain, and hurt. Our society gravitates toward movies that give the message one can not only be all right, but excel, no matter what happens to someone. Underneath this lies a message that we must be all right at all costs; the more that has happened to us, the more we should do to cover it up, pretend it's not there, and whitewash ourselves to cover up any trace of darkened damage from our lives.

Yet in the middle of an epic love song, we find someone who says she is "dark, but lovely." She's not trying to be anyone other than herself. It's not about overachieving. By declaring herself such, she is acknowledging there will be bad days and moments where she tries to process her experiences with trauma. The lover she speaks to has the responsibility of loving her anyway — and he does. She's not perfect. She's traumatized. She's not one thing or the other, and definitely not whatever she was beforehand. She is dark, but lovely; dark and lovely; both/and, not either/or.

    No matter how dark our reality is, we are still both dark and lovely. It might take us a little longer to get there or require more of those to whom we are closest, but in darkness, we embrace both/and in a way that combines to create something beautiful.

THE TRUTH IS THAT LIFE IS DELICIOUS, HORRIBLE, CHARMING, FRIGHTFUL, SWEET, BITTER, AND THAT IS EVERYTHING.
(ANATOLE FRANCE)[13]

TWELVE

DAMAGED

THE RIGHTEOUS CRY OUT, AND THE LORD HEARS THEM;
HE DELIVERS THEM FROM ALL THEIR TROUBLES.
THE LORD IS CLOSE TO THE BROKENHEARTED
AND SAVES THOSE WHO ARE CRUSHED IN SPIRIT.
(PSALM 34:17-18, NIV)

READING: ISAIAH 53:1-10

SOME years back, the girl group TLC released a song called *Damaged*. It was not a huge hit for the group, probably due to the sensitive nature of the song. Such was conveyed through the poignant music video depicting the results of domestic violence in a woman's life. At the end of the video, the main character literally falls into pieces because her life has damaged her to the point where she falls apart. There's no denial, no pretending her situation is different than it is. Positive thinking won't change things, mantras won't change things, nothing will change the fact that, right now, as she stands, she is damaged.

When I started to emotionally unpack the trauma that was found in my marriage, I came to a point where I deeply identified with TLC's music video. Coming to accept that things were often far worse than I let on to the outside world (and often to myself) was a disillusioning process. In it, I began to feel very damaged. Being out of it wasn't enough; I did not feel like a victor. I had so many people tell me I'd feel like a new person or renewed, but that day didn't come. I didn't feel a strong sense of relief or empowerment...I felt, instead, like I had been so damaged from what I'd experienced, there was no hope for me. One realization led to another and yet another. Following each realization came with questions, curiosities, and the ultimate pondering: would I ever be all right again?

The answer as to whether I would be all right again is complicated. Damage is damage is damage. There is no way we can return to a period in our lives when we didn't experience it. The experiences that in, some way, damage us aren't easily erased from our memories (if such is even possible). I think the imagery presented in TLC's music video gives us a good idea of what damage is like: it feels like we lose little pieces of ourselves. One by one, those pieces fall off us, signifying our existence as we feel ourselves falling apart. We stand back and grow deeply in touch with the parts of us that are now missing, feeling the results as we are left standing limited, with nothing left to us that matters. We don't feel ourselves anymore.

While damage can't be undone, our lives can be reassembled. Sometimes this is as difficult a concept as damage by itself; what comes together will be very different from what we remember. We learn that pieces can be gathered; they can be glued, or taped, or gold embossed, to bring us to a new place of togetherness. There is evidence of the damage, but we can still hold ourselves together. It often comes in forms we never imagined: being able to function day-to-day when we want to fall apart, handling our regular business, doing our chores, getting through the painful days as best we can. One day, we feel ready to take bigger steps such as relationships, friendships, and needed changes that will bring us to a better place. We acknowledge we are still damaged, but the reality of damage doesn't feel the same to us. Just like once we saw our lives differently through the lens of damage, so too we will see our damage through a different lens of life.

When one has experienced damage, their lives aren't marked by becoming better than one used to be. It becomes a profound victory to be able to say, "I survived, and I am here." Life is no longer about competing with anyone else. It is all, in its entirety, about standing: reassembled, holding together, and exploring life from the perspective one now has in the aftermath.

But O, how bitter a thing it is
to look into happiness through another man's eyes.
(William Shakespeare)[14]

THIRTEEN

How I Didn't Get Over

> Blessed *and* enviably happy [with a happiness produced by the experience of God's favor and especially conditioned by the revelation of His matchless grace] are those who mourn, for they shall be comforted!
> (Matthew 5:4)

Reading: Psalm 73:21-28

My late husband had been gone for about three weeks when someone first mentioned to me the need to "get on with my life." From that point onward, I received multiple messages from people about an expressed need to "get over" or "get past" the loss I experienced through his death. It turned into an unspoken "push" within myself; I needed to get over the fact he had died and start doing whatever it was they all thought I should be doing again. What I should be "doing" varied based on the person; it could have been an expectation about dating, remarriage, work, social activities, or my ability to function day-to-day. It felt like in a whole new area of my life I wasn't measuring up, all over again.

The people who pushed for such things didn't understand the true complexity of grief. Grief isn't just one feeling or emotion; it is the feeling of everything that ever was colliding with what will never be. In grief, one can feel happy, sad, angry, lost, hopeless, disturbed, frightened, empty, lonely, and beyond, all at one time. One doesn't easily walk away from its complex sense of darkness. Expecting that someone just one day "gets over" grief is not only unrealistic, but empty.

In my own experience with grief, I battled recounting my life with my husband as much as I did his death. That is what people often don't get about grief — it wasn't just his death that was painful, but the process of my life with him. Now that he was gone, I had to find some way to find peace within myself. There would never be a resolution either way to the things left undone. There, I came to understand that grief isn't something we ever "get over" or "get past." It is, instead, something we learn to live with as we go about our days.

If we recognize grief isn't something we "get over," that becomes precisely the point. It's perfectly all right we don't "get over" it. It's a game changer, something that makes us different. In grief, we must become different because we must adjust to an entirely new way of being. It's not something that ever passes away or ever leaves our minds. We learn to live with it; we adjust; and we go forward, best as we can, with where we are, now.

I describe the loss of grief like this: Imagine your favorite dish at a restaurant. You've tried other things on the menu, but none of them are your favorite. A big part of the reason you go to this restaurant is because of that dish. Then, one day...they take your favorite dish off the menu. You're crushed. You don't know what to do or think, because the major reason you went to that restaurant was for that menu item. Then, one day, you go back to the same restaurant, and you order something else. The experience isn't quite the same, but you find a new option that is good. You didn't get over anything but learned to live with the change.

I've done the same thing myself: I have learned to live with the change. It's a million different things on different days. Some days, it's better than others; on other days, it's so hard, I don't know if I function through them. I find myself relieved knowing there is no prize at the end of the grief experience. It's not about getting over but experiencing life in a different way. My lens, my perspective, my view from here is different. It's not better or worse, but I sit, and through grief, learn in a larger way to accept life on life's terms. And no matter what anyone thinks of it, what I am doing and how I am handling life is perfectly all right.

LIFE IS ONLY A LONG AND BITTER SUICIDE,
AND FAITH ALONE CAN TRANSFORM
THIS SUICIDE INTO A SACRIFICE.
(FRANZ LISZT)[15]

FOURTEEN

Human, All-too-Human

> Humble yourselves [feeling very insignificant] in the presence of the Lord, and He will exalt you [He will lift you up and make your lives significant].
> (James 4:10)

Reading: Romans 3:21-31

I'VE heard it said that we are no closer to the divine than when we are in touch with our humanity. This is not to indicate that we, as human beings, are God; we assuredly are not. What this does tell us is that the limits of human experience are designed to make us aware of just how much we need God. Situations that draw out our inadequacies echo our need to seek something greater than ourselves for resolution. Difficulties call us to God; away from the best of humanism and failed human ideas unto something deeper, more eternal, and more profound.

I never felt God closer in my life than when my late husband was dying. Even though I felt close to God, I hated every minute of it. It tapped into my own inner nature of inadequacy; one that tells me I can't do anything right, I am not enough, and I am not who is needed at the right time. I felt God in that place because I felt so limited, so powerless to do anything about the situation I faced. I was experiencing, as I call it, "powerlessness that changes me." It caused me to seek something more from God than the superficial things I might have often asked Him to do. I sought, I prayed, I endured. I waited. I felt like no one understood.

I felt limited.

I felt...human.

As I experienced these limitations, I found a profound truth I wish I'd known years earlier: When we reach out in our need, we come to discover that God often doesn't change the immediacies of our situation, our pain, or our emotional angst. He lets us feel our humanity, those limitations we have as human beings. God gives us a chance to dive deep into our feelings, exploring new places within ourselves and the mental and emotional states we didn't know existed. In the beautiful darkness, we go on a journey that drives us closer to Him, gaining insight into spiritual things that we would otherwise never experience.

Many believe God's purpose to be one by which He spares us from every touch of life, emotion, strong sense of difficulty or pain, because He is our comforter. They forget that in emotional release and journey we come to discover true comfort; a sense, a reality of the presence of God that transcends our human limitations and our often-trite concepts of divinity. God goes from our extreme perceptions: a God in the sky waiting to punish us at any turn, One totally devoid or uninterested in humanity, or one protecting us from the bad in the world as if we live in a bubble, to a God that is real; real in our suffering, real in our pain, and yes, real even through the tumult of that nature within us that is so human, it connects us to Him.

As human beings, we like the illusion of unlimited potential. We will get behind any idea that tells us we can imagine ourselves as more, greater, and better than we are right now. It's appealing to think we can transcend the painful things of life if we try hard enough. Just as

Satan desired to ascend to the heights on his own thanks to his own imaginings, we like that idea for ourselves, too. Our painful, tiresome, emotional states make us realize our limitations: we cannot, no matter how much we might try, supersede our humanity. In some moments of life, it will be that humanity that saves us, as it makes us realize we can't do this life thing, this death thing, or this eternal thing without our Savior.

Severe truth is expressed with some bitterness. (Henry David Thoreau)[16]

FIFTEEN

BLESSED SILENCE

Let be *and* be still, and know
(recognize and understand) that I am God.
I will be exalted among the nations!
I will be exalted in the earth!
(Psalm 46:10)

READING: ZECHARIAH 2:10-13

WE live in a world that thrives on noise. In modern times, it's easier to avoid silence more than ever in history. Cell phones, playlists, tablets, social media, internet sites, live streaming, computers, and television monitors infiltrate our lives, forming background tracks full of alert notifications, songs, shows, opinions, and thoughts. While there's nothing wrong with music, entertainment, or sound, the fact that our lives are often permeated by a sense of noise and distraction speaks powerfully of avoidance. I believe part of the reason we seek out constant stimulation is to keep from thinking deeper thoughts, especially in times when we don't want to think about anything that causes us to realize we aren't where we want to be.

Eventually our noise quiets to deafening silence. In the dark of night, we find ourselves in the hush of nothingness. Rainy Sunday afternoons find nothing on television and long pauses of quiet reflection. The Wi-Fi goes out, leaving total silence. Suddenly, in that deafening silence, we find ourselves confronted with everything we avoid, and more. We discover all the things we feel, we need, we seek, and that we need to know and release unto God.

We've all seen Psalm 46:10 on T-shirts, keychains, Bible covers, and coffee mugs, but we don't quite get the complete meaning of the passage in our English translations. The passage isn't just telling us to be still and know about God, but to be still and know God. If we want to know God, we must acknowledge the original Hebrew terminology for the words "be still" are "let go." Our command is not just to be still, but to stop moving, stop being distracted, stop finding and seeking noise, confront our haunts, and trust God with them.

It is in blessed silence – not silence for no purpose, but silence for purpose – that we come to find the need to let go of the things we avoid. In so doing, we express our trust in God. We take our cares, our worries, our hurts, our pains, and our grief, and we give them to the One Who doesn't patronize our experience in exchange to receive the blessing of peace.

I believe we fear confronting our deepest pains because we don't know who we will be without them. When we hurt for a long time it's easy to think we can't be ourselves if we rest them at God's feet and receive His rest in return. The noise we seek externally echoes our own thoughts and fears, an internal chaotic wall that separates us from feeling the things that hurt the most. That's why it's no accident that God doesn't just ask us, but commands us to stop – to be still – so we can let go. We stop and hit the wall, tearing it down, inviting us to His safe space where we don't have to fear the pain and grief of life that we carry.

There is a blessing in silence. There is a blessing in discovering God in a new way; a way that transforms how we perceive our relationship with Him as well as how we perceive ourselves. Through the lens of silence, we are bound to God Himself; we are no longer bound to our hurt. We experience divine exchange in the place that no one else knows nor experiences, because it's just between God and us, as His children. God does amazing things in the place of nothing, in the place of creation whereby light is called from darkness.

In noise, we find distraction. In silence, we find our freedom. In God, we find our hope; our faith; our empowerment. In silence, we find God.

WE SWALLOW GREEDILY ANY LIE THAT FLATTERS US,
BUT WE SIP ONLY LITTLE BY LITTLE
AT A TRUTH WE FIND BITTER.
(DENIS DIDEROT)[17]

SIXTEEN

THE GOD WHO SEES MY MISERY

> THE ANGEL ADDED, "I WILL INCREASE YOUR
> DESCENDANTS SO MUCH THAT THEY WILL BE
> TOO NUMEROUS TO COUNT."
> THE ANGEL OF THE LORD ALSO SAID TO HER:
> "YOU ARE NOW PREGNANT
> AND YOU WILL GIVE BIRTH TO A SON.
> YOU SHALL NAME HIM ISHMAEL,
> FOR THE LORD HAS HEARD OF YOUR MISERY.
> (GENESIS 16:10-11, NIV)

READING: LAMENTATIONS 3:19-26

HAGAR'S presence in the Bible is often overlooked. The modern-day church treats her much like she was treated in her day: as if she was a second-class citizen, only present in the story as a collective detail. She's forever stigmatized with the mistakes of Abraham and Sarah, regarding both her and her son as mistakes themselves. I often think of Hagar's experience and wonder what it must have been like to live in her situation: subjugated as a sexual slave, forced into a relationship with a man who was literally decades older than her, only to have a child that wasn't going to be hers until he was replaced by a full biological child. Then, when things got too hot at home, Hagar runs away, only to be sent back. The second time, when sent away with her son, she has to forge an entirely new way of being with no societal status, as a single mother.

Then I step back and realize I know what it's like to live in someone else's shadow. I know what it's like to be cast aside in favor of someone else. I know what domestic violence is like. I know what sexual violence is like. I know what it's like to not know where to turn, what to do, or where to find the next answer. I know what it's like to cry out to God in a fitful state, and hope somewhere, someone recognizes my misery.

Hagar is in the Bible for many reasons: she teaches us about welcoming outsiders into the family of God, considering those that society might consider of "less estate," and that just because a situation isn't ideal doesn't mean God can't use someone mightily, despite misuse and abuse. But there's one important reason I believe Hagar is part of our family of faith, one we don't easily consider...In her pain and misery, God saw her. God was just as much with her when she had the supposed child of promise as He was when her child — and familial status — was quickly replaced and reproved. He saw her when she was hurt, when she was frightened, and when she was alone. He saw her, and He loved her, even in the midst of her grief.

Hagar didn't see the angel of the Lord (often considered a revelation of God Himself) when she was happy and content. The angel of the Lord appeared when she was at one of her lowest, aching points, cursing her situation and fearing for her future. She came to know the "God who sees," as she called Him, in her misery. It meant more to discover God in the deep, dark place than on the mountaintop; it brought her to a place where she recognized the foreign gods of her people have no ears to hear, mouths to speak, or emotions to care. She found empathy, a realization in the true God, and knew that whether it was going back to submit to a household that didn't care for her or having to forge life on her own,

Hagar was in the hands of One greater who knew all she experienced.

    Life doesn't afford any of us the convenience of avoiding pain or difficulty. Every one of us will find ourselves crying out in misery, hoping there will be someone on the other end who will help us resolve it. We might not find the results or conclusions we always seek, but we will find the God who sees our misery. Instead of sweeping it under the rug, He, too, will acknowledge that's what we experience and is part of living life this side of heaven. We will live Hagar's theology, coming to know that God is as real as any pain and misery we might face. In such, we learn that even if He doesn't take us out of it, He is mighty to comfort without becoming condescending. Our pain is as real to God as it is to us.

Remorse sleeps during prosperity but awakens bitter consciousness during adversity.
(Jean-Jacques Rousseau)[18]

SEVENTEEN

Mourning in the Abstract

> Oh, that I [Jeremiah] could comfort myself against sorrow, [for my grief is beyond healing], my heart is sick *and* faint within me!...
> For the hurt of the daughter of my people am I [Jeremiah] hurt; I go around mourning; dismay has taken hold on me. Is there no balm in Gilead? Is there no physician there? Why then is not the health of the daughter of my people restored? [Because Zion no longer enjoyed the presence of the Great Physician!]
> (Jeremiah 8:18, 21-22)

Reading: Lamentations 1:1-11

WHEN we talk about pain and grief, Jeremiah isn't a Biblical character we often reference. We are quick to think about Job losing...well...everything, Naomi and Ruth losing their families, Jesus in the garden before the crucifixion, or the disciples after the crucifixion (but prior to the resurrection), but we never think about Jeremiah's intense experiences as being grief-filled. We look at Jeremiah and say to ourselves, "Jeremiah was a prophet! Intensity is part of the job!" We regard his prophetic work as if it was something he put on at the beginning of the day and took off at the end of the day, sunning himself on a rock somewhere with a cocktail in hand after the prophetic work was completed. Jeremiah is treated as if his grief, his message, and his feelings had no validity outside of his job to deliver a message.

We act like his feelings didn't matter because they weren't neatly compartmentalized and easily identifiable.

we skip Jeremiah because, perhaps, Jeremiah makes us uncomfortable.

Jeremiah was called the "weeping prophet" because his intense call broke his heart. As he looked over the state of Israel in his time, Jeremiah felt the loss of his nation: impending captivity and occupation, the unfaithfulness of the people, and the suffering that was to come. I believe he felt his prophetic doom more deeply than someone else might have because he didn't have anyone in his life. Jeremiah didn't marry or have children as part of his prophetic call, and that means as he heard from God, dictated divine words, and proclaimed the message, he did so alone. Distractions were harder to come by in Biblical times; he couldn't put on Netflix, scroll down Twitter, or go to the movies for the afternoon. Day in and day out, Jeremiah felt the message he was called to proclaim to a nation that didn't want to hear it.

Jeremiah's call left him an outcast. He lived rejected by his peers, alone and distant, knowing what was to befall an unfaithful people. He mourned perpetually; not because he lost a spouse, his ministry, or because he experienced a natural disaster...but because there wasn't much else for him to do. The depths of his deep, deep sorrow were so abstract, and so often intangible at that point, all he could do was feel it.

When we hurt, our experience often reaches a point where it is as intangible as Jeremiah's was. Sure, initially people might be able to connect or "see" what is upsetting us, but grief and hurt reach a point where we might not even know what is wrong within ourselves. We feel something: out of sorts, sad, weepy, unhappy, disconnected, and we don't understand why. By this time, people assume whatever was wrong isn't now, and we can't readily give voice to our process. We feel like Jeremiah did, mourning over something abstract, something just out of reach, that others can't see and don't understand.

    I believe part of the reason we see Jeremiah's experience in a first-person narrative detail is to show us about the world of intangible grief. It is grief that is so many things and yet nothing, all at the same time. God wants us to know that mourning the abstract is as real as any other form of grief or hurt, and that it does matter. Whether we mourn for something personal or something bigger than us, God is there with us in that process. It is appointed for healing: the healing of ourselves, of our people, maybe even our world, as we realize things such as grief – and feeling – and hurt – are often bigger than we, ourselves may be.

THE SENSITIVE ARTIST KNOWS
THAT A BITTER WIND IS BLOWING.
(HERBERT READ)[19]

EIGHTEEN

THERE IS HOPE FOR A TREE

For there is hope of a tree, if it be cut down, that it will sprout again, and that the tender branch thereof will not cease. Though the root thereof wax old in the earth, and the stock thereof die in the ground; Yet through the scent of water it will bud, and bring forth boughs like a plant.
(Job 14:7-9, KJV)

Reading: Revelation 22:1-5

WHEN we think of bitter, grief-filled periods, we seldom think about growth. Most people consider them to be places where we get stuck, and rightfully so. It's not uncommon for those of us who experience grief and loss to feel stagnant for long periods of time. We don't feel like we are moving forward or backward, and growth is often the last thing on our minds. We are stressed, overwhelmed, and so consumed with what we feel, we don't realize what is happening to us. In those states of unbridled emotion, we are growing out of the world as we know it into something else.

Trees aren't common images of grief, but they teach us much about it. Just as a tree might be cut down, it can come back to life, on its own, in its own time. The roots remain, giving the tree time to dive deep into its recesses so it can grow again. The new branches shall sprout, without fail, proving that new life has returned where it was once lost. It's part of nature's intricate design; one that displays a grandeur of growth's powerful truth: it is often slow-moving. We can't see it, we don't recognize it, but in the end, we do discover it for ourselves. Walking a step or two at a time, sometimes moving back, and often moving in a circular motion, we learn to follow growth's lead instead of expecting it to move the way we desire.

One of the reasons why grief and long-term sadness make people uncomfortable is because it isn't a fast process. There is no way to fast-track grief and cram it into a weekend or a few days. It moves at its own pace, slowly paving the way to a slow-growing, slow-moving hope that sprouts as a hewn down tree. Grief hurries for no one; not those who are left behind, nor those who might be uncomfortable with its chronic way of recoloring life as one knows it.

Just as there is hope for a tree, there is also hope for us. The quiet hope we come to find resting within us as grief ravages isn't hope that we often stereotype, loaded with optimism and positive outlook. It is the assurance of cyclical reality: the truth, both in eternity and nature, that life is cyclical. Things die and end, only for other things to begin and start again. In the process, we find ourselves feeling things both familiar and unfamiliar at the same times. In some ways, we don't wind up all that far from where we begin. The non-binary experience of grief shows us that life doesn't stop because we are "hewn down." It's not one thing or either/or; it's everything, something that connects us to life and eternity at the same time. Life is stronger than its challenges, and eternity is greater than what we see at any given time. Grief connects us to life; it connects us to eternal truth; and it proves that life, in its cyclical manner, always gives us a sense of true hope.

I believe we see the process of grief in a tree to teach us that growth isn't always fast, nor always visible to others. Life has a way of cutting us off. It's not measured by the final product, but the slow process that brings about new life. Life's cycles don't move rapidly, but one season at a time, consisting first of minutes, then hours, then days, then weeks, and eventually, months. The seasons remind us of the beauty in beginning; periods of work; harvest; letting go; and rest. From season to season, our tree changes shape, form, color, and design, displaying growth in ways we don't recognize in an immediate sense. It's raw and complex, beautiful and promising, all at the same time. Just like grief's process is; just like hope is; and ultimately, just like life is. There is hope for a tree because there is hope for us.

I WILL SEE THIS GAME OF LIFE OUT TO ITS BITTER END.
(ZANE GREY)[20]

NINETEEN

THE SPACE BETWEEN

AND WE ARE SETTING THESE TRUTHS FORTH IN WORDS
NOT TAUGHT BY HUMAN WISDOM BUT TAUGHT
BY THE [HOLY] SPIRIT, COMBINING *AND* INTERPRETING
SPIRITUAL TRUTHS WITH SPIRITUAL LANGUAGE
[TO THOSE WHO POSSESS THE HOLY SPIRIT].
(1 CORINTHIANS 2:13)

READING: 1 JOHN 3:15-20

THE Space Between was a huge hit for Dave Matthews Band. It was illustrated in its dark but powerful music video that brought the literal feel of "space between" to life. The video holds an air of tension, discord, and disagreement in its awash grayish, urban and industrial feel. Its depiction feels raw: it feels real, as you feel the tension...the awkwardness...and the true experience of "the space between." The song accurately captures the reality that the space in between things: people, ideas, relationships, goals, thoughts, feelings, and emotions, is often wrought with tension.

In life, we spend a lot of our literal and mental space in "the space between." Things happen and we feel the results of them. We then live in that place...that tension, where we experience our situations, feelings and losses, up close and personal. In between what we express and what we don't lies that space between, the place where we process all that has happened. As we wrestle, as we struggle, and as we experience the world of conflict, we come to experience something deeply profound: the truth.

"Truth" is often spoken of as an absolute binary: something that fits into a nice, neat category. I think that as much as we discuss it in theory, we don't understand it in reality. While it is certainly true that there are absolute truths, we are quick to throw the idea of truth around as if it's a nice, neat weapon we can use against others and often against ourselves. We believe facing the truth will clean up messy things, enabling choices to be easy and circumstances to be different. We pontificate. We are condescending to the challenges others face. We make judgments, both casually and with virulent force. "Truth" is our divider, our standard; something we use to exalt ourselves and cover up who we are underneath our superiority complexes.

Then something comes along which forces us to experience truth rather than muse its ideals. We can't control it and we live with it...in it...through it. There we find ourselves in the "space between," revealing ourselves to not be as much as we exalted ourselves to be. Truth doesn't come as a weapon, but a reality that snuggles up close and personal to us in a way we'd rather it wouldn't. It lies underneath the feelings we have that cover up its reality: anger, indifference, judgment, scorn, and yes, bitterness. We reject it at first; it is too uncomfortable to receive. It makes us see ourselves in a deeper way, as well as changing the way we see the entire world. It's no longer black and white, binary in polar opposites. It is suddenly awash of color, splotches of gray here and there, revealing nuances of life that make truth more than just a mere musing. In truth, we discover reality; in reality, we discover that life is often not quite as simple as we make it out to be.

In the "space between," we adjust to the discovery

of truth. Truth finds us, meets us, and we become acquainted with its sense of profound insight and revelation. Its powerful gaze stares into us, and we stare back into it, to find more of ourselves. It's a place of transformation, not in the sense that is fun or makes us want to run around the church, but one that creates a profound change in one's perception of self and others. Life becomes that sacred space between where we might be and where we want to be (also known as reality): one that doesn't need excessive words or thoughts, but somehow...just understands.

I FEEL LIKE EVERYONE HAS BEEN IN A BITTER SITUATION, REGARDLESS WHETHER IT'S CHEATING OR JUST NOT BEING OVER SOMEONE WHO IS OVER YOU — YOU COMPARE YOURSELF TO THE NEXT.
(ELLA MAI)[21]

TWENTY

WHEN YOU HURT...BUT CAN'T TELL ANYONE

You number *and* record my wanderings; put my tears into Your bottle—are they not in Your book? Then shall my enemies turn back in the day that I cry out; this I know, for God is for me.
(Psalm 56:8-9)

Reading: Jeremiah 15:15-20

It is possible to become so focused on healing the preoccupation with such becomes toxic. It's not uncommon to hear "folk therapy" applied to painful situations, often that inflict further pain and cause people to feel hopeless. We are told that we can't move on or have the fullness of what God might want for us in the state we are in, because we don't "heal" from it. We are told we aren't finding relationships because of whatever it is we give off; we can't meet new people because we are "too needy;" or that things aren't getting better because we aren't "healed." The question becomes: "What does being healed look like?" There is so much pressure to seem all right – be all right – and feel all right with things that have or are happening in life, even if you don't feel that way about them.

As a result, there are many of us (me included) who've felt the need to draw within ourselves and keep our hurts to ourselves. It feels like there is no one safe to tell, because no space has the sanctity to guard our pain. When people push healing as if it is an unobtainable thing, something that must be done now "or else," people's pain becomes a secret, buried force that surfaces to hurt, time and time again.

Healing shouldn't hurt in the sense of causing additional trauma and pain. While there are times when confronting and dealing with certain things is clearly difficult, healing shouldn't be used to hurt those who need to receive it. Healing isn't a singular destination, a weapon, or an idea meant to cause additional trauma. It is something designed to set us free, leaving us able to accept, rather than expect our experiences to be different than they were.

Healing is seldom a once-and-done occurrence in our lives. The things we face, the emotional hurts and haunts, the mental wounds, and sometimes even our physical ailments are layered throughout our being. We don't just wake up one day and stop experiencing hurt. Even if we successfully overcome one thing, there will be something else, at some point in time, that will require our need for healing, once again. That's why we speak of healing as a process: it is something we walk through as we learn to look at our experiences differently. There will forever be a reason to do this, reframing our personal feelings to adjust our perspectives to reality. We find language for what happened to us and narration to understand it in context, accepting it for what it is. The second we feel like we hurt and can't tell someone else, the longer the process becomes.

It's been said that secrets kill, as feelings buried alive never die. It has also been said that shame dies when stories are told in safe places. Both statements are true, revealing the truth that hurt needs to speak its truth to heal. The deeply personal nature of hurt, pain, and grief requires safety for its expression, not pressure.

There should be no place where healing becomes unsafe, nor where it is unsafe to speak one's healing process.

The very nature of hurt demands that we do tell someone about it. Doing such is the catalyst to begin our process: admit something is wrong, something doesn't make sense, something happened. When we give it language, we can give it clarity. In clarity, we can see our way to something better; ultimately, the freedom from our internal bondage that has, for ages, kept us silent.

But truly, I have wept too much!
The dawns are heartbreaking.
Every moon is atrocious and every sun bitter
(Arthur Rimbaud)[22]

TWENTY-ONE

ROSES

[SHE SAID] I AM ONLY A LITTLE ROSE
OR AUTUMN CROCUS OF THE PLAIN OF SHARON,
OR A [HUMBLE] LILY OF THE VALLEYS [THAT GROWS
IN DEEP AND DIFFICULT PLACES].
(SONG OF SOLOMON 2:1)

READING: RUTH 4:13-15

WHEN I first started growing roses, I tried growing them indoors – like I did with most of my other plants. I assumed that would be all right because I bought the roses at the same store as several house plants, I could do the same with small rosebushes. To my great chagrin, the roses would never bloom again. The plants often looked brown and on the edge of death. I started to assume the roses we bought at the store were just duds, and maybe weren't grown to last from season to season.

That was until I talked to my best friend, a rose enthusiast, about their condition. The first thing she told me to do was put them outside. Her advice was clear and direct: roses don't like it inside; they are not an indoor plant. I was horrified, as it was nearly winter in North Carolina and the idea of taking a plant and putting it outside in the winter seemed...wrong. I did what I was told though and put my near dying mini rosebush outside. I figured at this point, I had nothing to lose.

Not only did that rosebush not die... it flourished. It regenerated itself, growing in new places, developing new leaves. It wasn't long before it bloomed. Since that first plant, I've been able to acquire a few others who have all made their home on the side deck of my house. They never come inside. I watch them grow and flourish from season to season: pruning in late winter, growing leaves, fighting aphids in the spring, and blooming all year — as late as November and December.

My mom pointed out recently that you'd think roses would be delicate because they are often associated with things deemed fragile in life: relationships, love, beauty, gentleness, and romance. In watching our roses, however, we have found things to be the exact opposite. Under the right conditions, roses display great resiliency. When one cane is done, another one bursts forth. They withstand harsh conditions. Roses weather all seasons, through their changes and their unique challenges. They don't just grow one way and are done. Roses are resilient because they keep growing in different ways.

As I look over my roses, I believe they teach us that life, love, relationships, and even hope are possible after we've been left for dead or are near dead. We are stronger than we think if we are willing to grow in different ways. We should be fragile and delicate, but we are not. Our bitterness gives us the ability to be stronger, to see things differently. We have dwelt in the state of pain in all sorts of seasons, leaving us open to knowing more of what is coming, just by virtue of experience. We've experienced the pain of pruning, of being cut back so much, we feel we are reduced to nothing. It's a process that is painful, an experience that is neither enviable, nor desirable. The truth is, however, that it is necessary.

We love to admire the beauty of a rose, but we don't consider what it goes through to be beautiful. For that rose to stand in its glory, it goes through tough realities; it goes through life. It loses branches, petals, blooms and leaves, eventually losing much of itself as seasons require its change. Yet in the harshness of its conditions, it flourishes. Nobody can understand its miraculous manner of growth...and everyone stands back and marvels as it blooms in the middle of December. This, my friend, is the product of its loss.

I VENTURE TO PROPHESY THAT THERE LIES BEFORE US
A BITTER AND AN EVIL TIME.
(AUBERON HERBERT)[23]

TWENTY-TWO

COMFORT ME

Comfort, comfort My people, says your God. Speak tenderly to the heart of Jerusalem, and cry to her that her time of service *and* her warfare are ended, that [her punishment is accepted and] her iniquity is pardoned, that she has received [punishment] from the Lord's hand double for all her sins.
(Isaiah 40:1-2)

Reading: John 14:16-20

THE evolution of what I classify as "conceptual theology" is a fascinating examination into the way that humanity's relationship has changed with God over time. Conceptual theology is the manner in which individuals perceive God from a personal perspective rather than an "on paper" theological musing. In such a study, we examine what we coin as the "personal relationship" with God and the way people see God for themselves. It examines the way external factors (natural disasters, blight, illness, social reform and societal changes, occupation, and cultural shift) influence relationship with the divine and perception of such, especially as people respond to those various external factors. It is the connection between experience and spirituality; the place where human beings recognize their limitations and seek something deeper...something eternal, something comforting...to resolve their personal angst.

When the Israelites experienced occupation in intertestamental times, they found themselves in a place where their concept of God was challenged. Israel was officially occupied and scattered, with many of the nation's inhabitants in diverse places. The Jews in this time felt isolated and alienated, far from God and one another. As they cried out to God, they realized they didn't need to feel the harsh, cold, impersonal tinge that the Law often left them to experience. They needed to feel a warm, loving presence, one of a God Who was as present with them in their occupational disobedience and isolation as in their brief and fleeting periods of obedience.

The result of their search is what is now known as the "Shekinah," a concept often translated as "glory." Shekinah is more than just a mere concept of spiritual radiation, however. It is considered the dwelling presence of God on this earth, one that envelops and invites, reflecting a female presence of a mother gathering and comforting her children. In their pain, their loss, and their contemplation, they came to discover an essential aspect of the nature of God: God as Comforter.

When we experience trauma, loss, grief, or all the above, we find ourselves the same situation as Israel was, as is mentioned above: we want to be comforted. We want to feel a touch of something that lets us know our pain and our hurt are seen by someone else. Traumatic experiences make us feel invisible; all we want is to know someone, somewhere sees us, for what we are and what we experience. Even if someone doesn't understand it all, we take comfort – knowing we are seen – in that connection.

In Christianity, we understand the Holy Ghost to serve as our "Comforter." The work of the Spirit in our lives leads us into a place where we know, sense, and experience the true presence of God for ourselves. Even though we can't see God, we can sense His presence, knowing that God is with us in our heartache, as our Comforter.

The experience of comfort leads us to comfort others, as well. When it's our turn to stand in need, someone stands in that space: prompted by the Comforter's love, they too provide a reflection of eternal comfort. When someone else is in need, we do the same. The touch, the reality of comfort changes us, leading us back to the eternal presence of God, always at the moment when we need it most.

I HAVE BEEN BACK IN PARIS FOR TWO WEEKS.
NOTHING NEW.
LIFE IS STILL BITTER
(CAMILLE CLAUDEL)[24]

TWENTY-THREE

RESOLUTION

> ONE GENERATION GOES AND ANOTHER GENERATION
> COMES, BUT THE EARTH REMAINS FOREVER.
> (ECCLESIASTES 1:4)

READING: PSALM 144:1-4

SOCIETY talks a lot about the abstract concept of closure, especially for those who have experienced something involving grief or loss. The concept of closure holds that through a specified ritual, you can find needed conclusion for unfinished situations: a memorial or funeral, writing a letter to a loved one and burning it, discussing things with someone who has hurt you for the last time, or some other practice designated to close what's still left open from an emotional perspective. Lack of closure is often cited as the reason why people have a hard time moving on after difficult experiences. People might reconnect with a toxic ex in their lives, find themselves feeling stuck or voided, or engage in self-destructive behaviors. We are told closure is the answer to solving these problems. If we do the ritual, we will find that part of our lives closed, and, therefore complete.

But what happens when we do the ritual – or all the rituals – and we still don't find ourselves feeling complete? It is entirely possible to express all the feelings, throw all the crumpled requests in the roaring fire, scream as loud as we want, attend the formal service, scatter the literal or metaphorical ashes, complete the process, and still feel things are unfinished. We can still feel hindered, unable to move forward or backward. It can still feel like something is lacking or missing.

In many situations, we think we want closure when what we really want is resolution. We find ourselves at a juncture in life, usually one we didn't ask for nor anticipate. We don't care about whether the situation has closure; we want the situation solved to our satisfaction. We want to feel our feelings matter and that the situation we are in can be fixed in a way that will heal our broken, hurting hearts. A vague ritual doesn't seem to be enough. Forgiveness doesn't even feel like enough. We want to stop hurting. We want whatever was done to be magically erased. We don't want to be in touch with our own anguish any longer. We want the feeling of resolution: things are no longer painful, no longer hurtful, and all has its place, as God rests in His heaven and all is right with the world.

The problem is life seldom leaves us in situations that offer resolution. More often than not, we find ourselves left holding complex emotional bags full of a complicated mixture of feelings not so easy to identify. They run together, weaving deep combinations of roots that sprout new thoughts, feelings, and ideas within us. It's a huge adjustment to look out over life, seeing things through this wounded perspective, and know you seek something that will most likely never be resolved in this lifetime. We hope for it. We long for it. And, in our deepest moments, we know that longing is insanity, even though we don't know what else to do.

Ritual can be a great thing when it comes to seeking a sense of finality to a situation, but this is very different from the sense of completion human nature seeks as it tries to resolve the "bigger picture" of hurt that has transformed us. Now, we learn to take things one at a time: learning new things about ourselves, our thoughts, our feelings, our perspectives, the new way in which we see everything...even life itself. We learn to move with grace, not in a cheap sense, but recognizing how much we need a divine spiritual presence to get us through our ups, downs, and ultimately, days.

WISDOM IS LEARNED THROUGH EXPERIENCE,
AND SOMETIMES EXPERIENCE IS HARD AND BITTER
(LEO SAYER)[25]

TWENTY-FOUR

I'M NOT OK AND THAT'S OK

> AT THE EVENING SACRIFICE I AROSE FROM MY DEPRESSION, AND, HAVING RENT MY UNDERGARMENT AND MY MANTLE, I FELL ON MY KNEES AND SPREAD OUT MY HANDS TO THE LORD MY GOD, SAYING, O MY GOD, I AM ASHAMED AND BLUSH TO LIFT MY FACE TO YOU, MY GOD, FOR OUR INIQUITIES HAVE RISEN HIGHER THAN OUR HEADS AND OUR GUILT HAS MOUNTED TO THE HEAVENS.
> (EZRA 9:5-6)

READING: ECCLESIASTES 12:1-7

ONE of the first messages I ever preached was titled, "I'm Not OK (and That's OK)." I didn't realize it at the time, but it was a groundbreaking message in a day when people did not discuss mental health issues from the pulpit in a thoughtful manner. I got the inspiration for the message because back then, I struggled with my struggle related to chronic depression. I would go to visit churches and people would talk about being positive and upbeat, casting down things such as depression as demonic and "of the devil." We were given the message that if we had enough faith, we wouldn't have things such as depression or hopelessness anymore. This echoed much of the pop psychology back in the day: the goal of "feeling" things was to get over them so we didn't feel them anymore, as if there were some sort of feelings switch we could turn on and off. Underlying the message was clear: feelings were "fine" as long as we didn't have them anymore. This equated, at least in my mind, to the message that feelings are bad, and we need to get rid of them.

It hurt to learn that people felt I didn't have enough faith because I couldn't kick depression. More than hurt, it made me feel like I was a bad Christian. When I looked over the pages of the Bible, I couldn't find anything that told me I had to be positive all the time. There was no verse that mentioned depression was a sin, nor were there any that indicated it was demonic to experience periods of depression. Then I found the book of Lamentations – an entire book dedicated to long-versed poems about the pain of loss and grief in times of occupation.

Something in me clicked when I read Lamentations; it was not only OK to not be OK...there were times when being "OK" would have been deemed inappropriate. It would have been inappropriate to be optimistic and upbeat as the city of Jerusalem was ransacked by invaders, people were forcibly removed, and destruction surrounded its inhabitants. The people were supposed to lament; they weren't to skip through the streets and sing praise songs. They lamented because that was a normal, reasonable feeling to experience in the midst of such overwhelming realities. They weren't OK and that was OK.

Lamentations reveals to us that periods of grief and sadness in response to traumatic events aren't just normal...they are also godly. The entire expanse of human emotion can find itself rooted in the faith experience, and not just so we can "get over" our feelings and no longer have them. In every emotional response we have, we find God speaking to us: revealing things about Himself, about ourselves, about the world around us, and about the way life comes together on its own terms, in its own way. We feel constantly, whether we feel everything, or nothing, or something in between. Lamentations proves to us as it moves through different stages of grief that there is room for every feeling we have. None of them take away from, nor invalidate our faith.

It's been a long time since I first preached that message. In the years that have come, I've still experienced periods of difficult emotional processing including more chronic depression, Post Traumatic Stress Disorder, long brushes with grief and sadness, extreme frustration, and general feelings of inadequacy, failure, and loss. The difference is I am learning, as I go through the years, that such is all OK. I am not a bad Christian because I hurt. How I wish I'd learned that many years earlier.

I LOVE PLAYING THE BITTER GUY.
(BILL ENGVALL)[26]

TWENTY-FIVE

BEAUTIFULLY BROKEN

My sacrifice [the sacrifice acceptable] to God is a broken spirit; a broken and a contrite heart [broken down with sorrow for sin and humbly and thoroughly penitent], such, O God, You will not despise.
(Psalm 51:17)

READING: 2 CORINTHIANS 10:12-18

WHEN my husband first died, I was so busy handling situations (arrangements, memorial, sorting through personal items, moving, illness, and then the loss of one of my dogs) I didn't have much time to feel anything. That state of comfortable numbness was, admittedly, familiar to me. As a long-time leader, conventional standards told us to keep our feelings and issues drawn, lest anyone recognize or know we might be going through something. I knew how to hold it all together, maybe better than most I knew. The state of being required to maintain so many moments, days, and events of perfect togetherness was exhausting beyond measure. Yet the way it became second nature to me was, in hindsight, scary to confront.

What I didn't know how to do was fall apart. When this happened one day, I felt nothing short of confusion. I went from desiring to preserve the memory of a man I had a complicated relationship with – like a stereotypical "good little minister" – to a confused, divided mess. I thought I was doing good with his death and that I was all right with the life we led, only to discover

I was not in the least. I had no idea how jaded much of my life left me. I suppose that when we go through things for long periods we break, and break, and break again, not realizing the effects until we are in different situations.

Many question why we go through the experiences of trauma, grief, and loss in this world. There are those who believe that if we are in God, we should not have these experiences. As I described in an earlier devotion, our brushes with the more negative aspects of life exist to connect us to God because our humanness limits what we can do in such situations. We learn who we are, and in that process, we learn who God is, for ourselves.

Our breaking points destroy our pride.

We love to ride on top of the world through our emotional highs and hide our lows. We hope everyone sees our good times: that they take note of where we are and our great successes. It's easy to think we got there on our own, through our own extraordinary powers and abilities. It's also easy to forget about God as we bask in the glow that seems to be, feels like, and is extraordinarily marked with...us. No matter how things might start to go wrong, we do our very best to maintain the appearance that we are, as we think, the masters of our destiny.

Then something comes along that breaks us – literally and figuratively. We can't hold it all together anymore because there isn't anything to hold. We find out the keen, clever way in which we relied on ourselves isn't sufficient any longer. Now, we stand, broken: in need of comfort, healing, soothing words, and the love of God and others. For this point, we are now beautifully broken; fallen apart, into little, jagged pieces that suddenly let light pour in where we'd kept it out.

    We have these experiences for that reason: to break us. There is nothing beautiful about pride, but there is something amazing about breaking through to humility. To know God, we must first know ourselves, fully acknowledging our own limitations. In pain, in loss, in grief, we know who we are and what we cannot fix. Our sorrow, our loss, and our pain cannot be resolved if we hold it all together, ourselves. Then we come to know, in a much deeper sense, the One Who can fix what we cannot, as we learn to daily embrace the beauty in brokenness.

On a good day, I'm a bitter, angry, chip-on-my-shoulder type of guy.
(Dolph Ziggler)[27]

TWENTY-SIX

Dry Places

Yet I am the Lord thy God from the land of Egypt, and thou shalt know no god but Me: for there is no saviour beside Me. I did know thee in the wilderness, in the land of great drought. According to their pasture, so were they filled; they were filled, and their heart was exalted; therefore have they forgotten Me.
(Hosea 13:4-6, KJV)

Reading: Exodus 13:18-22

A few years back (more than any of us care to remember) my friend Julie Harvey authored a book called *Big Valley*. In it, she discusses the spiritual "valleys" in one's life and finding God in those difficult junctures. There was one thing she pointed out in the book that has stuck with me through the past few years: the word "Zion" means "dry place." "Zion" was a term used for the city of Jerusalem and, by extension, for the land of Israel as well. It was an appropriate nickname for both: they are desert locations, noted for a sense of dry, barren, emptiness.

Theologians have contrasted the realities of Zion with the promises God made to the Israelites. It wasn't, in a natural sense, a land overflowing with "milk and honey." It was a desert, complete with mountains, valleys, limited water, rugged terrain, heat in the summer, cold in the winter, and a great feeling of emptiness. God personally brought Israel to Zion, promising it would be a certain way...yet it doesn't appear to have the qualities promised. Knowing God, this wasn't without purpose. What lesson was He trying to teach them?

God took Israel into a dry territory that was unknown to them. Just as He had led them through the "dry place" of the wilderness, He was going to lead them through this experience. Here, they would have to work harder: explore the land, make a living, grow their own food, learn the terrain, and learn life all over again. Here, the place would be dry for the same reason it was dry in the wilderness: they were to remain focused on Him without distraction. Just as much as in their transitional period, they needed their "dry place" to make sure they weren't chasing everything around them in favor of forsaking His direction.

We often associate places of "promise" with abundance. It is our belief that being in a place of fulfillment will look like it overflows with milk and honey from the outset. When we are brought to a dry place, we can easily wonder what God is doing in our lives, and why. We can rest assured, however, that in a dry place, God is doing exactly what He did with the Israelites. He has brought us here to speak the things that are not as though they are, giving us the perfect environment to both heed His voice and watch Him work.

Dry places are obviously barren; lifeless; and empty, at least on the surface. No one would think them to be the site of miracles, promise, or the bloom of renewed life itself, but that's exactly what they become when we use them for their purpose. God takes us to dry, difficult places to show us what He can do through and with us if we will only trust Him. As we walk their breadth and height, it can seem impossible to fathom that anything will ever come of this dry emptiness but more dryness and more emptiness. Yet here we learn about trust in a way we never could have imagined. God takes us through impossible, dry, impassible places because He is the God of the impossible. We learn this nowhere more than as our lives reduce us to dryness. Here, we find He restores us from places when such seems unfathomable. What we think can't happen is exactly what God does.

We think we can't experience comfort. We think we will hurt forever. We think this is the definite end. We roll in the dry place, waiting to hear from God. One day, God answers. Amid our dry surroundings, we find the abundance we've sought and wrestled for, and life and love move forward.

I'VE TASTED THE BITTER BEATINGS.
(CHRIS EUBANK, SR)[28]

TWENTY-SEVEN

BRAVE ENDINGS

> BETTER IS THE END OF A THING THAN
> THE BEGINNING OF IT, AND THE PATIENT IN SPIRIT
> IS BETTER THAN THE PROUD IN SPIRIT.
> (ECCLESIASTES 7:8)

READING: MARK 14:66-72

THE Apostle Peter was known as the "Zealot" prior to his ascent as a church leader. He acquired this nickname because he identified with a revolutionary political party that sought to conquer the Roman Empire by Jewish revolt. It was their belief that if they could call the people of Judea to bear arms and fight against Rome, Rome would have to leave Judea.

On the surface, this might sound like a great plan, much like the way we handle things today: let's just go in, siege, and charge, right? The problem was that it wasn't a "beginning" that the Zealots had any chance of successfully launching and finishing. They were merely rebels: they knew how to start trouble, how to start conflict, and how to start the spread of plans...but they had no way to finish them.

Peter had zeal — he had passion — he had wild, burning fire within him — and it wasn't getting him anywhere in his life because it wasn't properly tempered. It was just a crazy combustion that led to a lot of out-of-control behavior that earned him a reputation. He knew what he hoped for and longed to see — the Kingdom of God come — but he was going about it all wrong.

It took the loss of Jesus through the crucifixion to bring Peter to his own end. As Jesus was being crucified, Peter denied Him not once, but three times. Watching the end of his leader brought Peter to a point where he had to deal with his own concepts of "kingdom" and the idea that what he wanted to bring about was not going to be a reality. It forced him to look at himself. It forced him to look at his behavior. No matter how ideal what he wanted might have been, he wasn't doing things right. Behind all those "beginnings," behind all those burning passions, behind all that wild behavior, there was nothing more than promises unkept.

The death of Jesus made Peter and the other early apostles and believers markedly brave. By accepting His death, they were able to see the hope and promise in the new era that would follow after His resurrection. It was Peter who stepped up on Pentecost to handle a confused and insulting crowd, eloquent to educate them through the gift of interpretation of tongues with the power of the Gospel. In Peter's loss, he gained something; he gained a sense of bravery and an empowerment for a true new start, a true new beginning, that would help him to come to discover and embrace the Kingdom he believed and sought out all along. He was no longer just a rabble rouser without a cause; his experience with an ending made him brave.

It's hard to stand out over an experience marked by tremendous loss and say it's supposed to make us brave, but that's exactly what it does. In beginnings, we find motivation; in endings, we find purpose. In the bravery purpose provides to us, we find freedom. Our losses give us the courage to stand up where we should, walk away from what no longer works for us, and some way, somehow, find ourselves again.

In loss and grief, we find exactly what we are made of because it takes bravery to face the unfairness life has thrown at us. We are forced to accept endings, admit things are over that we often weren't ready to see end, and come face-to-face with ourselves in pain, in sorrow, and sometimes, even in places of grief or shame. There, and only there, do we find what the journey has been about the entire time.

It's one thing to be bitter about something,
but it's another thing
to recognize the growth
and the change that you made.
(XZBIT)[29]

TWENTY-EIGHT

STOP WAITING FOR FRIDAY

> Can your heart *and* courage endure or can your hands be strong in the days that I shall deal with you? I the Lord have spoken it, and I will do it.
> (Ezekiel 22:14)

READING: GALATIANS 6:9-11

A recent move of mine left me feeling overwhelmed and hopeless. Even before I moved, I found myself drowning in all my "stuff." I am going to describe it with that nondescriptive term (which used to drive my junior high English teacher crazy) because that's just what it was: "stuff." Clothes, shoes, purses, little things we collect over the years, books I didn't like or wasn't going to read, jewelry that gave me a rash, hats I wasn't going to wear, and more...stuff.

The past several years had kept me from doing a regular cleanout like was needed. Even before the events of the past few years, I hadn't done a good one — a comprehensive one — in a while, at least not for my personal items. Once my husband died, I had to handle the cleanout for his items, shifting the focus off my own. Then there was the first move, done under duress. When the time came for the most recent move, it was also under duress, but for different reasons. It was my resolve that with this move, I would tackle the household of "stuff."

I successfully tackled some things. Some of the situation was aggravated by a mold infestation in my closet, forcing me to give away items I probably shouldn't have moved in the first place. When time ran out, many more things were moved that probably should not have been. When I moved, I found myself surrounded by boxes, both with things I needed and things I didn't.

I tried to address the situation at hand in different ways, all of which left me feeling overwhelmed. Everything I tried triggered my grief: losing my husband, losing my dog, losing friends, the changes in my ministry work, and leaving the place I called home for ten years. I couldn't believe my life had come to this: boxes full of things that formed memories too difficult to process in bulk. I resolved to leave everything where it was until I was better able to handle the emotional response this project had now triggered.

The new problem was I now had boxes everywhere, triggering another response within me. I had to live now; I couldn't wait for something magical to come along and make me feel less grief stricken. I counted the boxes in my room and started unpacking one box per day, tackling maybe four or five things at once instead of forty. Slowly, one thing at a time, I was able to feel better.

When we grieve, we spend our entire lives waiting for "Friday" to come: the day when we will have something to which we look forward and enjoy. We think our emotional pain will be resolved in an external thing: something that shifts our focus, the calendar date, or an event that will suddenly cause us to feel differently than we do. Nobody tells us that living "one day at a time," in each moment, can hurt. We long for something to come that will take us out of our moments and launch us into something better.

Problem is, the mysterious "Friday" will never arrive.

Sure, we will feel better intermittently, but we will never find our solution to the pain of life — and the adjustment of reliving — if we always wait for something else to carry us to a different place. We must do the hard work. We must feel it, process it, and learn where to go from here.

The thing that will make us feel really good? Having the courage to emotionally unpack: to live, to feel, and to confront again, even if it's only one box at a time.

> I am a greedy poet.
> I keep munching life all the time.
> Sweet, sour, and bitter moments.
> (Gulzar)[30]

AFTERWORD

LEARNING TO LOVE THE BITTERNESS

Blessed be the God and Father of our Lord Jesus Christ, the Father of sympathy (pity and mercy) and the God [Who is the Source] of every comfort (consolation and encouragement), Who comforts (consoles and encourages) us in every trouble (calamity and affliction), so that we may also be able to comfort (console and encourage) those who are in any kind of trouble *or* distress, with the comfort (consolation and encouragement) with which we ourselves are comforted (consoled and encouraged) by God. For just as Christ's [own] sufferings fall to our lot [as they overflow upon His disciples, and we share and experience them] abundantly, so through Christ comfort (consolation and encouragement) is also [shared and experienced] abundantly by us.
(2 Corinthians 1:3-5)

When I wrote my book, *Waiting: Devotions for the Journey*, I never intended to write a follow-up or companion volume. I figured I'd write that book and call it done. When I found myself still struggling with the same issues over a year later with the same issues – only in a more intense manner – a companion volume came to me one day while walking my dog. I was trying to process very intense feelings, ones that didn't seem to go away, no matter how much I might have tried to make them vanish. I was wrestling with how I felt. I was wrestling with what I felt my life had become. I was wrestling with both interior and exterior conflicts. I was fighting myself.

At one time, I thought the emotional and spiritual burden of my husband's death would be magically lifted from my shoulders and I'd feel like an entirely new person. When I examined my own thoughts and feelings deeper, I realized the dark, melancholy, pessimistic way I viewed the world wasn't exactly a new phenomenon in my life. I'd always edged toward such a view; it was just far more prevalent now. I wasn't someone whose optimistic worldview was suddenly interrupted with grief. Instead, I was someone who now had experienced enough of life to have my views both reinforced and justified.

What this period – and this book – have helped me to do is come to a better place of acceptance and understanding of this part of myself. Much of the time, life doesn't afford us a "silver lining" to our dark clouds. That's part of life's dark purpose: it serves to mature us, to see things, not from an incessantly positive view, but from a perspective of insight. We need to be people whose message is taken seriously in every concept and idea of our lives. The sobering, life-altering changes that come out of nowhere cause us to straighten up: we can no longer go through life in states of blissful ignorance.

In sorrow, we discover what matters. In grief, we learn what to value. In loss, we learn to treasure what is truly important. In lack, we learn gratitude. At every juncture of the bitter, negative aspects of life, we learn true values that help us find meaning not just in a place of nothingness, but throughout our lives, long-term.

Bitterness is bitterness is bitterness. It is raw, real, and unhinged, and takes us to mental and emotional places we never thought possible. It brings us face-to-face with life itself: the casual way our plans and future visions find themselves disrupted in a manner that's beyond our control. Nothing can cause it to backtrack, nor can anything overcome it. We learn to live with it and within it: sometimes struggling, sometimes accepting, but always, figuring it out, in steps we'd often rather not explore.

We hate it and yet we still rise to the challenge, day in and day out, because life continues, even when we don't want it to do so. The way we rise isn't always understandable to others and that's all right, too. It's not about us and them anymore, but about sorting out a reality that leaves us feeling anything but optimistic. No longer naive, no longer condescending, and no longer dripping with platitudes, we see the realities of life forever changed. We've sat in the dark so long we squint at the light. And the difference now, that changes us forever, is we are easily willing to sit in the dark with someone else because we've become fluent in the deep, dark silence that only melancholy can provide.

References

[1] Hudson, Saul; Stradlin, Izzy; McKagan, Duff; Reed, Darren A.; Sorum, Matt; Rose, W. Axl. November Rain. https://www.google.com/search?client=firefox-b-1-d&q=November+Rain+lyrics. Accessed December 13, 20201.

[2] Strong's #048483. *Brown-Driver Briggs' Old Testament Hebrew Lexical Dictionary*. https://www.studylight.org/lexicons/eng/hebrew/04843.html. Accessed December 23, 2021.

[3] "Bitterness Quotes." https://www.brainyquote.com/topics/bitterness-quotes. Accessed December 28, 2021.

[4] Ibid.

[5] Ibid.

[6] "Bitterness Quotes." https://www.goodreads.com/quotes/tag/bitterness-quotes. Accessed December 28, 2021.

[7] Ibid.

[8] Ibid.

[9] "Bitter Quotes." https://www.brainyquote.com/topics/bitter-quotes. Accessed December 28, 2021.

[10] Ibid.

[11] Ibid.

[12] Ibid.

[13] Ibid.

[14] Ibid.

[15] Ibid.

[16] "Bitterness Quotes." https://www.brainyquote.com/topics/bitterness-quotes. Accessed December 29, 2021.

[17] "Bitter Quotes." https://www.brainyquote.com/topics/bitter-quotes. Accessed December 29, 2021.

[18] Ibid.

[19] Ibid.

[20] "Bitter Quotes." https://www.brainyquote.com/topics/bitter-quotes_2. Accessed December 29, 2021.

[21] Ibid.

[22] Ibid.

[23] "Bitter Quotes." https://www.brainyquote.com/topics/bitter-quotes_3. Accessed December 29, 2021.

[24] "Bitter Quotes." https://www.brainyquote.com/topics/bitter-quotes_4. Accessed December 29, 2021.

[25] ibid.

[26] "Bitter Quotes." https://www.brainyquote.com/topics/bitter-quotes_5. Accessed December 29, 2021.

[27] "Bitter Quotes." https://www.brainyquote.com/topics/bitter-quotes_6. Accessed December 29, 2021.

[28] "Bitter Quotes." https://www.brainyquote.com/topics/bitter-quotes_7. Accessed December 29, 2021.

[29] Ibid.

[30] Ibid.

Other Books Of Interest By The Author

- *A Heart God Can Use: The Journey to the Center of His Will* (Remnant Words, 2018)

- *Between the Porch and the Altar: A Journey Through the Book of Joel* (Righteous Pen Publications, 2016)

- *Manifestations of the Spirit: The Work of the Holy Spirit in the Church and in Your Life* (Righteous Pen Publications, 2019)

- *Power for Today: Practical Spirituality for Everyday Living (Volume 1)* (Righteous Pen Publications, 2016)

- *Seeds for the Season: 91 Days of Breakthrough* (Righteous Pen Publications, 2018)

- *Waiting...Devotions for the Journey* (Remnant Words, 2020)

ABOUT THE AUTHOR

THESE THAT HAVE TURNED THE WORLD UPSIDE DOWN
ARE COME HITHER ALSO.
(ACTS 17:6, KJV)

Dr. Lee Ann B. Marino, Ph.D., D.Min., D.D. (she/her) is "everyone's favorite theologian" leading Gen X, Millennials, and Gen Z with expertise in leadership training, queer and feminist theology, general religion, and apostolic theology. She has served in ministry since 1998 and was ordained as a pastor in 2002 and an apostle in 2010. She founded what is now Sanctuary Apostolic Fellowship Empowerment (SAFE) Ministries in 2004. Under her ministry heading Dr. Marino is founder and Overseer of Sanctuary International Fellowship Tabernacle (SIFT) (the original home of National Coming Out Sunday) and The Sanctuary Network, and Chancellor of Apostolic Covenant Theological Seminary (ACTS).

Affectionately nicknamed "the Spitfire," Dr. Marino has spent over two decades as an "apostle, preacher, and teacher" (2 Timothy 1:11), exercising her personal mandate to become "all things to all people" (1 Corinthians 9:22). Her embrace of spiritual issues (both technical and intimate) has found its home among both seekers and believers, those who desire spiritual answers to today's issues.

Dr. Marino has preached throughout the United States, Puerto Rico, and Europe in hundreds of religious services and experiences throughout the years. A history maker in her own right, she has spent over two decades in advocacy, education, and work for and within minority spiritual communities (including African American, Hispanic, and LGBTQ+). She has also served as the first woman on all-male synods, councils, and panels, as well as the first preacher or speaker welcomed of a different race, sexual orientation, or identity among diverse communities. Today, Dr. Marino's work extends to over 150 countries as she hosts the popular *Kingdom Now* podcast, which is in the top 20 percentile of all podcasts worldwide. She is also the author of over 35 books and the popular Patheos column, *Leadership on Fire*. To date, she has had five bestselling titles within their subject matter: *Understanding Demonology, Spiritual Warfare, Healing, and Deliverance: A Manual for the Christian Minister; Ministry School Boot Camp: Training for Helps Ministries, Appointments, and Beyond; Discovering Intimacy: A Journey Through the Song of Solomon; Fruit of the Vine: Study and Commentary on the Fruit of the Spirit;* and *Ministering to LGBTQ+ (and Those Who Love Them): A Primer for Queer Theology* (and its accompanying workbook).

As a public icon and social media influencer, Dr. Marino advocates healthy body image (curvy/full-figured), representation as a demisexual/aromantic, and albinism awareness as a model. Known to those she works with, she is a spiritual mom, teacher, leader, professor, confidant, and friend. She continues to transform, receiving new teaching, revelation, and insight in this thing we call "ministry." Through years of spiritual growth and maturity, Dr. Marino stands as herself, here to present what God has given to her for any who have an ear to hear.

For more information, visit her website at kingdompowernow.org.

www.ingramcontent.com/pod-product-compliance
Lightning Source LLC
Chambersburg PA
CBHW031646040426
42453CB00006B/227